There's more to dying than death

A Buddhist perspective

Lama Shenpen Hookham

Windhorse Publications

Published by
Windhorse Publications Ltd
11 Park Road
Birmingham
B13 8AB
United Kingdom

© Lama Shenpen Hookham 2006

Cover image: Eric Meola/The Image Bank/Getty Images
Cover design: Satyadarshin
Printed by Cromwell Press Ltd, Trowbridge, England

A catalogue record for this book is available from the British Library
ISBN-10: 1 899579 68 0
ISBN-13: 978 1 899579 68 6

Contents

For Michael

May the vast openness of the unknown,
That looms before you,
Greet you as the friend it has always been,
The indestructible essence of your being.

May the truthful mirror of death
That shines before you,
Dispel by its clarity life's fond deceptions,
Awakening the natural wisdom of your heart.

May the dark shadow of death
That falls upon you,
Unite you in terror with all life's creatures,
Touching the open wound gaping in the heart of your
    being.

May you find the courage to welcome
The thundering storm of reality
That is your being,
With the confidence of an ancient warrior,
Resting in the mysterious light of the timeless joy,
That knows no birth or death.

Lama Shenpen Hookham wrote this prayer for her brother
following his death.

Foreword

Life is precious.

It presents countless opportunities and challenges for discovering peace, joy, and truth from within ourselves. It also provides many opportunities to help other beings and to do something useful and beneficial for the world around us.

Death, from a Buddhist point of view, presents similar challenges and opportunities. It is neither the end nor the final judgement. It is another step on the journey with many special opportunities for discovering our true nature and thereby find lasting peace and happiness.

Shenpen Hookham explains the tradition and how to apply its teachings in the light of her own experience in the modern Western world. I have no doubt that all who read this book will find something valuable that they can carry with them.

Ringu Tulku Rinpoche

About the author

Lama Shenpen Hookham has practised Buddhism for forty years. In the 1970s she spent six years in India as a nun, and trained under Tibetan teachers such as Karma Thinley Rinpoche, Kalu Rinpoche, and Bokar Rinpoche. She has spent nine years in retreat and for the last twenty years has been a close student of Khenpo Tsultrim Gyamtso Rinpoche. Khenpo Rinpoche is one of the foremost living teachers of the Kagyu tradition of Tibetan Buddhism, a great scholar and master of meditation. On his instructions, Lama Shenpen completed a doctoral thesis published as *The Buddha Within*. He was so well satisfied with her understanding and meditation experience that he has encouraged her, as a lama, to teach Mahāmudrā. Her husband, Lama Rigdzin Shikpo, has also been one of her teachers for the last twenty-five years. His teaching has given her the confidence to express Dharma in English directly from experience rather that from texts. In this both she and Lama Rigdzin Shikpo have been greatly encouraged by their teacher, Khenpo Rinpoche. Lama Rigdzin Shikpo is a close student of the late Chögyam Trungpa Rinpoche, from whom he received Dzogchen teachings while the latter was in Britain in the 1960s. Khenpo Tsultrim Gyamtso speaks highly of Lama Rigdzin Shikpo as a Dzogchen practitioner.

Preface

This book represents an attempt to provide a Buddhist perspective on death that is both realistic and reassuring, for Buddhists and non-Buddhists alike, in facing bereavements and one's own death, as well as helping others to face theirs.

I have tried to focus on a perspective that a westerner with only a limited or, perhaps, no experience of Buddhist teachings will find helpful and reassuring, rather than assume the reader is an experienced Buddhist practitioner or has taken on board the whole Buddhist cosmology and world-view.

Accounts of death from traditional Buddhist sources can sound too technical and give detailed instructions on how to die that apply mainly to the most adept of meditators. This is likely to create unrealistic expectations for practising Buddhists who might not be confident in reaching the required standard of practice and become discouraged. Others might be alarmed by the warnings and descriptions of what can go wrong at death, so that, instead of learning how to face death with confidence, they become frightened by the thought of it.

So my intention is to give an account of the Buddhist perspective on death that will increase people's confidence and provide practical guidelines on what they can do for themselves and for others when the time comes.

To avoid becoming too technical, one might be tempted to make the Buddhist perspective on death sound simplistic. I have read so-called Buddhist accounts of death that imply that we just have to make our peace with everyone and quietly slip into the great blue yonder, as if all that is required is a peaceful death and all will be well thereafter. This seems to ignore the main thrust of the

Buddha's message about how difficult it is to escape the sufferings of the endless cycle of rebirth, and how the experience of
what lies beyond death can actually be very frightening.
Instead, such accounts make death itself seem to be the path that
leads to liberation from suffering. In fact, the Buddhist view is
that, unless we have Awakened to the true nature of reality, we
will take rebirth again and again, and our state after death is
quite uncertain. Just as dreams follow one after another, sometimes delightful, sometimes nightmarish, we just don't know
into what kind of state we will be reborn. So although advice on
how to minimize the sufferings of this life at the time of death is
important and useful, I am even more concerned to provide the
Buddhist perspective and guidance on what might be helpful
after this life has ended.

My presentation of Buddhism

The way I present the Buddhist perspective is based on the living transmission of the teachings I have received from my teachers and my meditation practice within the Mahāmudrā and
Dzogchen traditions of Tibetan Buddhism. These traditions
arose in India only about 1,000 years ago and flourished in Tibet,
but they are based on the classical Mahāyāna Buddhist scriptures, which give more or less identical teachings and can be
traced back to the early centuries CE. Essentially the same teachings can be found in the most ancient of Buddhist scriptures
going back 2,000 years or more, and are thus present (though
emphasized to greater and lesser degrees) in all the various traditions of Asian Buddhism. In general, I have not given much in
the way of references, and it may seem to some readers that I am
speaking on my own authority. However, I have in mind the
teachings of the Prajñāpāramitā sūtras on Emptiness, the teachings of the Tathāgatagarbha sūtras on the Buddha Nature inherent in every being, and the teachings in the *Avataṃsaka Sūtra* on
the vastness and interpenetration of all worlds. All these teachings form the basis for the Dzogchen and Mahāmudrā traditions
in Tibetan Buddhism. My teachers follow these teachings and
have transmitted them to me over the years.

Acknowledgements

Over the course of about ten years many of my students have had a hand in the production of this book, so I wish to acknowledge and thank them for all their help. I produced the book in response to students' questions about death, and it was initially an attempt to bring together the various bits of advice in one place.

The original booklet was called *Gateway of Death*, and was made available within the Awakened Heart Sangha in 2004. Last year Siddhisambhava suggested Windhorse Publications might publish it more widely since she found it such a useful book. The editorial board immediately took it up and ran with it, suggesting various changes to make it accessible to a wider public. The original was written for people already familiar with my style of teaching, nonetheless, even members of my family who knew nothing about Buddhism found it helpful.

Since I thought it would involve very little work to meet the editorial requirements of Windhorse Publications, I embarked on the process of preparing this version for them even though I was in retreat. My student Jonathan Shaw who was also in a year's group retreat with me at the time at the Hermitage of the Awakened Heart offered to help me with the project. Somehow, the more we looked, the more we found to do, and somehow the book fell apart and had to be put together again several times in the course of working on it. I hope the final product was worth all the effort. We certainly learned a lot in the course of working through the various aspects of the material.

I am particularly indebted to all my teachers, especially Khenpo Tsultrim Gyamtso Rinpoche and Lama Rigdzin Shikpo. I discussed particularly tricky points with my husband Lama Rigdzin

Shikpo, with whom I have worked for many years on how to teach Buddhism to westerners in our own language, following the advice and encouragement of Khenpo Tsultrim Gyamtso Rinpoche. He has told us that now we have a sound understanding of the profundity of the teachings for ourselves, we should try to express them to others in whatever language and terms make that profundity accessible to them. Some material is taken more or less directly from his own teachings on death and how it parallels the way awareness works in life. Finally, Ringu Tulku Rinpoche looked over the text and helped me with some difficult points concerning the actual death process and to what extent it matters what one does with the body after death.

So again I wish to thank everyone who helped to get this version of the book out: Siddhisambhava, Erin Ferguson, Dayden Palmo, Alice Lear, Agnes Pollner, and Cindy Cooper from the Awakened Heart Sangha, and Jnanasiddhi, Shubhra, Shantavira, and the all the team at Windhorse Publications. I especially wish to thank Jonathan Shaw for giving up precious retreat time to help me. I particularly appreciated his endless patience, insightful clarity, and tireless thoroughness in working through the text again and again, ironing out difficulties and unnecessary complications. I didn't always give him a very easy time!

Lama Shenpen Hookham
Hermitage of the Awakened Heart Sangha
May 2006

Introduction

Although the best time to read and reflect on death is before we have to face it – preferably a long time beforehand – few people do so. It is symptomatic of the human condition that life's preoccupations sweep us relentlessly on, leaving us with no time to think about death, and little inclination to do so. This is one reason why the prospect of death tends to come as a shock, when we are suddenly faced, at the worst possible moment, with fundamental questions about what life is, or was, all about. At that time, more likely than not, we will be scared, unable to believe what is happening, worried about doing the right thing, worried about how to avoid pain, worried about what we dare to hope for. Even when we have tried to prepare ourselves well in advance, death, by its very nature, still tends to come as a shock and can evoke emotions we scarcely knew were possible. It is very much with this situation in mind that I have written this book, hoping to provide guidance and reassurance in order to strengthen people's inner confidence for themselves as well as those around them.

In this spirit I have tried to present a Buddhist perspective on how to deal with the problems that confront us when we are faced with our own death or the death of someone close to us. I address the questions of what we can do to help, and how we should think and conduct ourselves in order to help ourselves and others.

In spite of Buddhism's emphasis on death, Buddhists can still find themselves feeling uncertain what to do when death strikes. In this book I have set out what I have found, over the years, to be the most important and straightforward guidance I could give when approached for advice. Even before they encounter death, I hope this book will provide Buddhists with a powerful reminder, and the means to make the thought of it a dear friend on the path to Awakening.

This book is also for non-Buddhists who are looking for a Buddhist perspective on death. I am approached from time to time by friends or family members of a dying Buddhist, who want some kind of context for understanding the needs and concerns of their loved one.

The importance of death in Buddhism
Death is central to Buddhism. It was the thought of death that drove the Buddha-to-be to abandon home and family to seek a path to liberation from suffering. In other words, he was seeking a place (or state) of safety that would not be shaken by death. So Buddhism could be said to be about death and the path that leads beyond it. It is important to understand that this perspective informs how Buddhists traditionally perceive every aspect of Buddhism, such as who the Buddha was, what state he reached, and how to reach that state ourselves.

The Buddha is seen not simply as a long-dead sage, but as an 'Awakened One', that is to say, someone who has awoken to a deep and timeless reality, in contrast with which our present understanding of life is like taking a dream to be real. The Buddha called that reality *Nirvāṇa*, which is peace, the ending of suffering, the heart's release. Significantly, it is also called the 'Unborn' or the 'Deathless'.

Historically, the Buddha was someone whose journey to Awakening began with the question of why, if we are simply to suffer death, are we born? He discovered the astounding truth

that birth and death are, ultimately, simply mistaken percep-
tions. This realization is referred to as Awakening or Enlightenment, as it is analogous to waking up and realizing that we have
taken our dreams to be real. The Buddha discovered that as long
as we continue to misperceive the true nature of reality in this
way, we take birth and die again and again, life after life. It is as
though we are trapped in dream worlds and cannot find our way
out. This state is referred to as *saṃsāra*.

The Buddha found a way, like finding an overgrown path
through the jungle, to step out of the confusion of saṃsāra into
the light and freedom of Nirvāṇa. That way is called the Dharma,
and it involves taming our hearts and minds in order to penetrate
to a deeper level of understanding of life and death through
reflection and meditation. Thus the Buddha's teaching gives us
the inspiration or hope of a goal for which to strive, and guidance
on how to reach it. However, to follow Dharma to its ultimate
goal, Nirvāṇa, beyond the reach of death, involves a long and
arduous struggle against our accumulated habits of thinking and
acting that keep us trapped within saṃsāra.

The good news is that even following the path of the Dharma to
some extent can bring immediate and profound relief, both in life
and at the time of death. Those who follow the path and provide
us with a living connection to it are called the Sangha. The living
connection the Sangha has with the Dharma has a power in its
own right, which protects, guides, and transmits understanding
to all those who have contact with it, both in life and in death.

For Buddhists, the fact that there is the goal of Awakening to
Nirvāṇa, the path of Dharma by which to reach it, and the
Sangha who show us that path, ensures there is always hope and
meaning in both life and death. Buddhists regard these as their
sure and abiding source of protection, whom they place their
reliance on by 'going for Refuge' to them. Thus going for Refuge,
the most fundamental and widespread practice of the Buddhist
tradition, has freedom from death as its ultimate hope.

Going beyond birth and death

It is understandable that those who do not believe there is any reality deeper than this life, and the death that ends it, do not want to dwell on the fact of death. But if you suspect there is a way to awaken to a deeper timeless reality that lies beyond birth and death, there is nothing more compelling than reflection upon death. Inspiration and joy can be found in doing so, since it turns one's thoughts away from attachment to what is unreal, and leads one in the direction of what is ultimately real and of lasting value. It is said to have lasting value because the true nature of our being that the Buddha discovered is one of genuine, unfailing joy, meaning, freedom, the cessation of suffering, and the endless power to relieve the sufferings of others, spontaneously and effortlessly.

Since we live in a secular society, there is a tendency for people to think of Buddhism as if it were just a method for calming the mind and having a more peaceful and fulfilling life here and now. People are looking for therapies and self-help programmes, and often come to Buddhism looking for nothing more than that. It is therefore tempting to present the Buddha's teachings as a kind of therapy: a way to learn to accept suffering, life, and death as they are, without trying to escape them. This fits in with the predominant view of our materialistic society in which to fear death, and to want to find a path that goes beyond, appears to be a kind of escapism. From this perspective, it seems senseless and morbid to spend one's whole life thinking about death!

It is true that the Buddha's teachings do help us to live our lives more happily. They help us to let go of our struggle to cling to the past or reject our present experience. This is well known to be the best way to reduce stress and anxiety and bring about a degree of mental peace. So the emphasis the Buddha placed on looking directly at our immediate experience can sound like a formula for a kind of hedonistic approach to life: one of enjoying the here and now and not worrying about the past and future.

From the Buddhist perspective, this is a short-sighted and unwise way of interpreting the Buddha's teaching, since it doesn't prepare us for suffering and death. When life comes to an end, one is left, like the Buddha, wondering what is the point of it all. It is important to realize that the Buddha's questions came from a deep love of life and his family and friends. He was not someone who had failed in life and wanted to run away. He saw that without a completely new understanding of the nature of reality, universal suffering is inevitable. His quest was to face this reality head-on. He was running from the false to the real.

What caused him to leave home in order to seek that reality was the thought that all his loved ones must age and die. That struck him as too tragic to bear. When he saw that all that is born dies, his question was whether there was, anywhere, anything of lasting value. Was it all a meaningless stream of fleeting events leading nowhere other than decay and death? If so, what was that pain in his heart that told him, 'No! There is more to life than this'? Isn't that our question too? The Buddha's answer was always to look within; to look into the true nature of our being.

Of course, one can shrug the whole thing off, and say that death is just part of life and nothing can be done about it. However, the experience of the Buddhist tradition is that it is deeply meaningful to pursue the questions that death throws into relief.

Who dies?

As in the case of the Buddha, it is more often than not the death of our loved ones and our own impending death that throws up these questions most urgently. Although Buddhism has often been understood to say that, since all is impermanent, death doesn't matter, and we should just accept it, it is actually saying exactly the opposite. It says that since all that we cling to as real is impermanent and ends with death, we should let go of attachment, so that we can find what is of undying worth. That which is of ultimate value is found in this very life, but it does not end with death. This raises the questions of what it is that dies, and what, ultimately, a person is.

Buddhism teaches that what is of ultimate value is the ungraspable mysterious essence of our being, which is present and accessible right now, and it is this nature in our ourselves and our loved ones that is ultimately real. The way some people talk suggests that they have an intuitive knowledge of this, even if they have no ready means of rationalizing it. For example, when we gaze on the dead face of someone dear to us, it is hard to believe that this corpse is the person we knew and loved. Similarly, many people have told me how they feel that some-one close to them who has died is still with them in a deep and undefined way. They may say something like, 'They are always in my heart.' I have heard people explain this by saying, 'Oh, they live on in our memories.' But this doesn't seem to capture it, as memories don't truly live and often do not last long. I think what is meant is that a person who has died lives on in our hearts as someone present and alive, much more than simply as a memory.

One could of course dismiss this feeling as mere fancy, but from the Buddhist perspective it makes complete sense. It reflects a deep and natural intuition about what our being is and how we are connected to others. It is this that gives us the sense of some kind of meaningful, living connection, and makes that dead body before us seem like a parody. It is not really them.

So the question is, what *are* we, really, deep within ourselves? In other words, what makes a person a person? This matters now, of course, in life, but it matters even more at death. If we can understand it in life, there is a chance we might be able to under-stand it at death.

The Buddhist tradition

Sometimes people say to me that they would like to believe there is more to us than what can be found under a microscope, but they are wary of religious beliefs that suggest there might be life after death. They make the point that just because it is comforting to think there is something that lives on after death, this doesn't make it true. I am impressed with their powerful allegiance to the truth, even if it's uncomfortable, and I think therein lies the makings of good Buddhists, because the Buddha told us not to accept things blindly, but to investigate them for ourselves by looking into our direct experience.

To start with, we don't know what is true, so we can easily be misled. Some of what we think of as knowing is actually deception. So the most important thing to investigate is how we know anything. The Buddha is renowned for having discovered that we have a deeper way of knowing than the one we usually employ when we are thinking. It is a more precise and all-encompassing way of knowing, not conditioned by thought. Until we find this other way of knowing, we cannot see what it is possible to know about the true nature of life and death.

Who has found that way of knowing, and how can we find it? From the Buddhist perspective, this brings us to the idea of the body of practitioners who follow the Buddha, who learn this way of knowing through meditation and can teach it to us. We are invited to try this out and see for ourselves whether this is true. At first, the truths we discover about ourselves might be far from comforting. That is why it is important to be committed to truth itself, whether or not it is comforting, if we want ultimate liberation.

Since death can come at any time, it might not give us time to discover much in the way of deep truths about the nature of ourselves or the universe. Does Buddhism provide any methods for approaching death that do not depend on our being advanced meditators with deep and stable realization of the nature of reality? The answer is yes. The Buddhist tradition has an abundance of methods to help everyone, whether they have faith in the Buddha or not, and at whatever stage of the path they happen to be. There are practices for all levels of understanding, and many ways of thinking, to give everyone protection, courage, and fortitude in the face of death.

Looking further, this path that the Buddha discovered is known as the sure path to the ending of suffering, not just in this life, but in all future lives, not just for oneself, but for all beings. This path is essentially one of training in order to discover what is of ultimate and lasting value in the core of our being. But although it is a path of training, it is also a living force, already accessible to us in the depths of our heart. We instinctively and intuitively know how to follow it; we just need to have it pointed out and we can turn to it with confidence as we face death. As it is a living force, it has the power to protect and guide us even into the unknown that lies beyond death.

Nothing can be said that will prove this, but what else do you have to turn to? In the end, we will just have to look into our own hearts, beyond the confusion of superficial thoughts, and see for ourselves what is truly real.

ONE

How meditation helps us understand death

To many, meditation suggests a process of relaxation to find peace and stillness within. But from the Buddhist perspective it is not a contrived effort to make oneself peaceful; it is a process of seeing accurately, so that we can step out of our fundamental confusion. All our sufferings, in life and in death, are caused by this fundamental confusion that prevents us recognizing our true nature. The remedy is to align with our true nature. First, we discover it through the process of meditation. Then, when we have learned to experience it fully and directly, we need to learn to trust it and rely on it, and in this way live and die with confidence and ease.

Thus Buddhism and meditation constitute a path of discovery by looking into our direct experience. Some people like to talk about direct experience, but when one investigates what they mean, it turns out to be no more than some kind of delusion or mere belief. Some people do not distinguish their religious beliefs from direct experience, and take this as proof of their beliefs.

I thought like this myself when I first encountered Buddhism. I wasn't looking for a religious belief system of any kind, because I already had Christian beliefs of my own. I was only interested in comparing notes, curious to see how Buddhist beliefs compared with mine. But what struck me right from the beginning was that the Buddhist view of reality was based not on mere beliefs, but on the truth the Buddha discovered for himself by exploring the nature of his direct experience. It was what was meant by 'direct experience' that really grabbed my attention. It began with something as direct, simple, and incontrovertible as 'the mind is fickle'. Here was something that I really did know for myself from my own experience; my mind didn't always do what I wanted.

I found it compelling that Buddhism was so connected with reality and the truth that it could take something as simple as my experience of my fickle mind as its starting point. I realized it was true as soon as I heard it, but I only discovered its real significance through the practice of meditation. I have since discovered that every shift, flicker, and movement of the mind tells us something and can be a means to opening the heart more and more. That opening of the heart can then reveal to us what is unchanging in our nature; a timeless reality that is not born and does not die.

Until I encountered Buddhism and meditation I thought that no one really knew, or could know, the truth about the ultimate nature of reality. But having encountered it, the possibility dawned on me that perhaps it had actually been discovered and that I could go to someone and ask them to show me how to discover it for myself. As a Christian, I had never been sure whether I was a sinner, or what God really was. There was always room for doubt. But here there was no question, since my mind was certainly fickle! I took up the challenge of exploring this and never looked back. I am still discovering things about my experience even more basic than the fickleness of my mind. In my experience, the more basic the discovery, the deeper and more far-reaching its significance and implications. I find this quite wonderful. We just don't know what we are missing until we look, and we don't think to look until someone points out that there is something of significance that is worth looking at.

This promise of a path based on complete honesty and attention to the precision of my own experience drew me into Buddhism there and then, and has held me there ever since It is this path that gives me confidence in the Buddha, the Dharma, and the Sangha, and it is this confidence that I intend to rely on when I come to die.

In this, I am following in the footsteps of the Buddha and his followers, who, out of compassion for others, have taught generation after generation of Buddhist practitioners how to follow the path of Awakening through the practice of meditation.

The fundamental nature of awareness

Meditation is the path of investigating and reflecting on our direct experience persistently, systematically, and deeply, integrating the fruits of those reflections into our lives. By doing this we gradually come to discover our true nature, and move forward on the path of fully Awakening to it. As our understanding and awareness deepens, our confidence in this, the profound nature of our being, grows. Whatever we are experiencing, however disturbing or frightening, however good or bad, we become better able to turn towards it with equanimity rather than trying to escape. This is the inner confidence that expresses itself as fearlessness in the face of both life and death.

In this chapter, I will explore how meditation can help us understand the nature of life and death. Through the meditation process we come to understand how, in a sense, we undergo birth and death over and over again during our lives, even from moment to moment, as we enter and emerge from thoughts and dreams. The death of the body will be a more dramatic version of something we are experiencing all the time. From the Buddhist point of view, the main difference is that at our physical death, instead of being reborn in a different moment of this life, we will leave this life and find ourselves in another life altogether.

All we know in life is our own experience. When we talk about life and death, we are talking only about experience. Death is the last experience of this life, and the Buddhist point of view is that there is no reason to think that experience does not continue after death. The fundamental nature of awareness, the basis of all our experience, does not change at death, any more than it changes from moment to moment in this life, thought to thought, dream to dream. The only difference is in what appears within it.

This is known by the Buddhist tradition through practising meditation and reflecting on our experience, by which we come to understand the fundamental nature of awareness. Having realized that awareness is fundamental and unchanging, we can understand how taking birth and dying are just appearances within awareness, like images in a mirror. This presents the possibility of passing from life to death without any problem. This truth can be glimpsed even in this life, and that glimpse could be enough to give us confidence in the path to Awakening. That confidence can then carry us through both life and death.

Getting caught in thoughts

What actually happens when we decide to meditate? We are given some meditation instruction, the essential point of which is that we are to keep awake and aware of our experience, whether it is of the breath or some other object. Why? Because, quite naturally, we wander off. So learning to come back again and again is a good exercise for noticing our direct experience of the mind. We cannot help but notice how we get caught up in one thought after another. Some of these may be happy thoughts about seemingly useful subjects, some are likely to be unhappy thoughts of anger or pain, but there are definitely a lot of thoughts appearing. As we become accustomed to this process, we can start to relax and wonder what it is all about. What are thoughts? What is this process of getting lost in them?

As we explore in this way, we can start to get an inkling of how this might be relevant to the whole question of birth and death. We see that each thought that arises is like a gate inviting us to go through into its world, which is like dying to one world and taking birth in another. There is usually a feeling associated with the thought that catches our interest. The feeling hooks us and, if we are not alert enough or determined enough, we pass through that gate and find ourselves simultaneously entering and creating the world that the thought has opened to us. That thought-world has its own storyline of the past and future, its own value system, its own flavour and mood. It has its own story of who we are, and we find ourselves identifying with that. We have taken birth in it!

At any moment we can choose to step out of that world, to die to it, and return to the breath, but it is surprisingly difficult. Having been born into that world, it is quite a wrench to pull ourselves out. It is like a mini-death. If just a thought can hold us so strongly, it is not surprising that life has such a hold over us. Of course, dying to thought-worlds in meditation isn't a perfect analogy for death. Death of the physical body is obviously far more traumatic than moving from one thought to another, because far more conditions bind us to this life.

Once we have been really hooked by a whole thought-world (like a daydream) we are so engrossed in it that it becomes our whole world while we are in it. Then, at some point, somehow, our intention to meditate reasserts itself. We notice we are not meditating, we are not being attentive and aware, and we have to make a move to bring ourselves back. It is very hard to say what exactly we do at that moment. Perhaps we could call it letting go. It is as if we let ourselves die to that thought-world. As we do so, we can choose to notice thoughts to be thoughts and not get caught up again, no matter how many more thought-worlds arise. In the same way, if we can recognize this world as just an appearance in awareness, we can let it go at the time of death, and not grasp any other world that appears.

Looked at in this way, we are experiencing a kind of death from moment to moment. We are having to die from the world we were in and take birth in the world of our meditation. Suddenly the past and future change, and we think, 'Oh, I have been away thinking instead of meditating.' But we were not away anywhere. Our fundamental awareness never went anywhere.

The Buddhist perspective is that, in the same way, when we die and take birth in another world, our fundamental awareness doesn't go anywhere. It does not have the nature of something that moves from place to place. It is like a mirror, unmoved by the images that appear in it.

The ebb and flow of awareness

In the above description, getting hooked by thoughts means focusing on a thought-world and getting sucked into it. Noticing that we are hooked and letting go is a kind of fading out or dissolving of that world. This process of focusing and dissolving that focus, ready to refocus, goes on all the time. It is fundamental to the nature of awareness that it does so. The whole process starts with a phase of sharp focus and a more or less stable involvement in whatever has appeared. Then there is a dissolution phase in which the focus relaxes and awareness becomes very spacious, and there is a strong sense of uncertainty. Then there is a complete fading out.

There is no reason to assume the same thing doesn't happen at death. We start from a focused involvement in this world, then there is the whole death process of that breaking down in a series of stages. Finally, as our connection with this life is sundered and we face the unknown, comes the phase of uncertainty. There is likely to be a surge of fear or panic at the immensity of this, and a sense of groundlessness. In this state of uncertainty just about anything can appear and there might be a rush of a multitude of appearances all at once. Then this experience also fades, and it is from this state that awareness begins to focus again, which is experienced as getting sucked into yet another world of some kind. This is rebirth.

From moment to moment, the same process is experienced, though less dramatically. As the focus on one thought relaxes, anything can appear in the gap. Then some kind of movement starts up and awareness is drawn back into a focused, stable involvement.

To understand this, you might like to try to catch a thought as it arises and ask yourself where it came from. This is a surprisingly challenging exercise and requires a teacher's guidance to really follow it through. What one notices, however, is that the thought suddenly appears, presumably out of awareness, but there was no awareness of anything when it arose. It would not be unreasonable to assume that in the same way, after death, a new experience can appear in awareness, seemingly out of nowhere, and carry us into a new world, a new life.

In life, each time there is a dissolution of a thought-world, a choice arises between recreating and entering the same world or creating a different world. At that time, various gateways or avenues of possibility may present themselves. This happens moment by moment, and we can become directly aware of this whole process as we meditate. Choices also appear at death, and we might try to perpetuate the life we have just left, but the conditions for birth have ended and we cannot get back. It is important not to try. It is best to let go, as though of a thought, and trust the unchanging nature of awareness itself as much as we can.

Lessons from dreaming

When, through meditation, we become better at staying awake and aware from moment by moment, we can try to notice this same process as we fall asleep. Falling asleep involves letting go of the sharp focus on the world of the senses. It is as if the world of the senses dissolves and we pass out or die to it. In that state of dissolution, awareness begins to move within itself and focuses again, but this time independently of the senses. Our awareness is full of countless gateways that open up into dream-worlds that it could focus on, enter, and get involved in. Thus it is that we find we are wandering from one dream-world to the next, as each dream-world dissolves and another appears. Without our being particularly aware of what we are doing, we get involved and enter one world after another. Our awareness is the creator of those worlds, as well as what enters and gets involved in them.

Even if we are unable to notice when we are dreaming, we can reflect on what happens in those dreams we remember and notice how this process is going on all the time. Anyone who pays close attention to their experience can notice this whole process. Meditation just means maintaining that close attention.

Since we can recognize this process in our direct experience whenever we realize we've been dreaming, perhaps it is not such a big leap to conclude that the same process happens at death, since our fundamental awareness doesn't change. However, at death the physical body is dying, so the connection between awareness and the world of the senses is being completely severed. We are not going to be able to return to our life as it was.

Our background sense of confidence

At the time of death, something quite basic to what we think we are is dissolving. This is our background sense of confidence about who we are and our place in the world. This confidence accompanies us through life and prevents us panicking but, in a way, it is a false kind of confidence. Nonetheless, it serves us well in practical terms, especially when we do not have the more fundamental confidence of being able to trust our true nature. This background sense of basic confidence stays with us throughout life, and is usually there when we are meditating and even when we are sleeping and dreaming. This is what allows us to fall asleep without being terrified. This is what enables us to remember who we are when we wake up. We are not usually aware of this basic confidence or that we rely so much on it. If we didn't have this, every moment would feel like death, it would feel like stepping into the unknown.

At death, this basic confidence is shattered and we feel we really are stepping into the unknown. Unless we have a more fundamental confidence in the true nature of our being, we will at that moment experience a rush of fear or panic followed by what we call passing out. In meditation, in order for that not to happen, we train ourselves to notice this false kind of basic confidence and learn to not rely on it. If we can do this in life, we are more likely to be able to do it at death. Then instead of a rush of fear and passing out, our heart can open and we could realize our own true nature right there and then. Death can be liberation, Awakening, Enlightenment.

Meditation is about letting go of a false confidence in being the person we associate with this particular time and place, and instead learning to rely on the simplicity of our true nature, which is not of the nature of something that is born and dies. It does not die, and that is why it is trustworthy. It is the ultimate refuge that the Buddha discovered.

Sometimes, as a result of meditation, it is possible for that ordinary background sense of security to be shaken by a strong experience of emptiness, a feeling of absolute groundlessness. It can feel as if one is dying, or as if one has indeed died. Worse still, it can feel like the whole of everything is dissolving or has dissolved, or even that it never existed in the first place. These are shocking experiences, as anyone who has experienced them will tell you. When fear arises in this way, it is because these are partial experiences of emptiness which pass pretty quickly, so we find ourselves back 'here', as we like to put it, maybe within seconds or within days. However, such experiences have much in common with the death experience. They illustrate how meditation can help us understand the death experience even in this life.

The moment of death and what follows it

What most of us do, most of the time, is identify with and attach ourselves to the worlds that appear in our awareness, and we come to rely on them as our home or our being. That is why we suffer when sooner or later we are wrenched away from them. This happens with dramatic totality at death; our connection with the world of the senses in which we have invested so much is completely severed. At that point we find ourselves exposed to the brilliance and intense sensitivity of the vast openness of our true nature, shining in our heart. But the chances are that we will be too terrified to experience that properly, and we will just pass out.

Although this intense experience is often called the Clear Light of the moment of death, and much is made of it, it's actually not much different from what happens when we fall asleep, or even from what happens as our awareness shifts from thought to thought. One thought finishes, another follows, and in between is a blank moment we cannot remember. The blank moment that we didn't notice is actually the Clear Light. Similarly, at death, unless we are an advanced practitioner, we do not remember the Clear Light experience of our true nature. You could say we are literally stunned by it, and then, after a while, we inevitably come out of that state, like waking from unconsciousness.

As our awareness becomes active again, new worlds start appearing in the unstable intermediate state that starts after one life ends and before a new stable life begins. In Tibetan Buddhism, this is called the bardo of becoming. From the Buddhist perspective, it is taken as given that lives follow lives just as dreams follow dreams and thoughts follow thoughts. The difference between a thought or a dream and a 'real' world is considered partly a matter of the stability of the world in which we take birth. A 'real' world would of course be shared with other beings in a way that our thought and dream worlds are not, but from the Buddhist perspective the distinction is not as hard and fast as we tend to assume.

So, as mentioned above, the intermediate state is thought of just like the unstable state when one thought-world has dissolved and we haven't quite settled into the next. The instability of the various worlds appearing and disappearing, when we come round in the intermediate state after death, occurs at tremendous speed, and this can be very frightening. Similarly, in meditation or just as you fall asleep, you may sometimes notice seemingly masses of thoughts or half thoughts flickering on the edge of your awareness. These are all possible gates or avenues into different thought-worlds, and the less stable we are, the more we are disturbed by those thought-worlds. Obviously, in the intermediate state after death, we are likely to feel extremely disturbed and buffeted about.

Meditation gives us a method by which to train ourselves to be able to wake up in the midst of thought-worlds and notice that we are simply thinking. Because this habit has developed in life, we can find ourselves, in death, spontaneously coming to and noticing we were caught up in our own thinking and letting it go. Whatever world appears to us is simply awareness focusing and moving within itself. There is always the possibility of choosing not to enter it.

All the experiences, frightening or otherwise, that drive or seduce us during the intermediate state between lives are actually occurring in our awareness. If we do not get caught up in them, they will just come and go like thoughts in meditation. To realize this would obviously save us a lot of suffering after death. As in meditation, it is a matter of recognizing that what is going on actually comes from awareness itself, it is our own mind, so we can let it dissolve without being swept along by it.

Meditation at the time of death

You might think the foregoing description of how meditation relates to death means that from the Buddhist perspective the only hope is to be able to meditate through the whole process of death. This would be rather depressing, since for most of us it's hard to meditate even with a heavy cold, so there seems little chance we will be able to meditate at the time of death. However, there is great benefit in having meditated in this life, even if realistically one is not likely to able to meditate well, if at all, at death.

If we have developed the habit of meditation over the course of our lives, we will hopefully have developed a certain degree of inner confidence, which will then carry us through whatever life or death throws at us. Even were our confidence to fail us at the time of death, the habits of mind produced by regular meditation will resurface spontaneously in the after-death state and in future lives. Those positive habits, such as openness to truth, equanimity, courage, and resourcefulness, will draw us repeatedly back to the path of Awakening, steadily deepening our understanding and increasing our confidence.

Perhaps even more importantly than any of this is that through meditation we are starting to cut right down to the source of our confusion, like starting to cut a tree down at its root. From the Buddhist point of view, it is our unskilful and harmful actions of body, speech, and mind that determine what kinds of worlds are going open up to us after death, and therefore what kind of future lives we are likely to have to suffer. But these actions and the habits that perpetuate them stem from deep-rooted confusion.

We could spend our whole lives trying to give up the multitude of bad habits, but it would be like trying to cut down a tree by hacking at its twigs and branches. A few axe blows to the trunk weakens the whole tree and causes the twigs and branches to wither. In this way, although Buddhism puts a lot of emphasis on the importance of skilful and wholesome moral conduct, the task of removing all our negative and egocentric tendencies would be endless if we had no means other than hacking at the twigs and branches, as it were.

The only real hope is to practise meditation. Not only does this undermine our negative habits, it also helps us to go further by deepening our understanding of the true nature of our direct experience, so that we can cut down the whole tree of confusion at its root. The good news is that every little movement of awareness that cuts through our confusion weakens its hold on us, so that life becomes easier and more enjoyable. Particularly, it can make a lot of difference to our confidence when the time comes to die.

The important message here is that from the Buddhist perspective, awareness, our fundamental nature, is unchanged by death. So at death, when all else fails us, we can still trust that our experience will continue and that we will be able to continue to relate to it as we do now. This in itself is not particularly reassuring, because who wants to endlessly experience one world after another if there's no meaning or purpose to it? The following chapter explains what it is that gives our experience a sense of meaning and connectedness, a direction that eventually leads to the bliss of Awakening that goes beyond all suffering.

TWO

The heart never dies

Traditionally, Buddhists emphasize impermanence and the illusory nature of this life at the time of death. This encourages us to let go of attachment to this life, and helps us open up to the path to Awakening. However, emphasizing impermanence only works, in the sense of giving people reassurance and confidence at the time of death, if they have a sense of connection to something deep and meaningful in people that is not going to die. Otherwise, emphasizing impermanence and illusion can sound as if one is dismissing any sense that a person has value in themselves. It can seem heartless and not reassuring at all.

But meditation on the Buddhist path is not only about impermanence and illusion. It is also about resting in the heart, the place where all hearts meet. This gives us the assurance that at death we are not alone, and that our loved ones do indeed live on in our hearts, even if we can no longer see them.

This again raises the question of what, then, is a person? The fact of death keeps throwing this question into relief. Are we really just a collection of chemicals or fleeting moments of consciousness that disperses at death? Our heart tells us that a person is more than that. But what do we mean when we say that? This is not an easy question, but the Buddhist path is aimed at discovering the answer, in all its fullness. In other words, what is impermanent and illusory about us is not what we are. We are awareness, and awareness is no other than our heart.

Thus the heart is the key to understanding what we are and the nature of our connection with others. It is through meditation that we can explore what a person is and what heart means. We discover how our heart connects us to other people and to what is truly meaningful within ourselves. This sense of connection and meaning is what we need more than anything else at the time of death, whether it is our own or that of others. Genuine understanding of the true nature of reality comes from being deeply connected with our heart through meditation.

To have a deep, ongoing confidence in our heart is the most important thing at death. You might be relieved to hear this, as the previous chapter might have left you thinking that you had to keep your mind lucid, clear, and focused. But anyone who has tried meditation will know how difficult it is to do that, even in good health, let alone when we are sick or dying. What we find is that our mind tends either to get too busy, or too dull to focus properly. This is very likely how we are going to experience our mind when the moment to die arrives.

There is a chicken-and-egg sequence going on here. Until we can create a gap in our busy mind, we hardly notice the heart, but once we start to settle in our heart, the busyness of the mind is no longer disturbing. Once the busyness of the mind is no longer disturbing, it is easy to settle into the heart and simply trust that. So meditation that calms the busy mind is helpful for settling into the heart, and settling into the heart helps calm the busy mind so that we can meditate. It is helpful to remember this at times of crisis, such as the time of death. It is not easy to do, but even to try a little can be a big help. Of course, the question remains as to what we actually mean by 'heart'.

Intuitions about the heart

We all have an intuitive sense of heart, and what it means to talk from the heart, even though we cannot really explain it. It is important to really explore all the associations we have with regard to the heart in this sense, because somewhere in there is a profound intuition. We cannot really say what we mean by it, except that it is meaningful and significant. It gives meaning to our whole life. A loss of heart means something like losing a sense of purpose or meaning, doesn't it? The worst suffering is always meaningless suffering, isn't it? It is worth pondering what we really mean when we say things like that.

From the Buddhist perspective, the reason we say and understand things like this, and what gives life meaning, is that the heart (in the sense we intuit it) is intrinsic to reality itself. The universe is not cold and meaningless matter. It is more like the heart that we intuit within us. What we sense as meaningful in our heart is really the living presence of the heart of the universe, right there in the heart of our being. That is a bold statement indeed!

From this point of view, heart is a long way from just a nice sentiment or a romantic idea. We are often guilty of sentimentality and romanticism, but we know this is not what it means to be true-hearted. When we talk about what we know in our heart, we are talking about what we really know, in the sense of what is of true significance and meaning. That is not just whim. From the Buddhist perspective, the reason it is not just whim is that it is an intuition that goes directly into the nature of reality. We are connected in the heart to the fundamental nature of reality that the Buddha discovered. We are in direct contact with it and we know it in our direct experience, even though we easily forget it or miss its true significance.

I suggest you stop and think about this for a minute or two. Would you say it is true that when you say 'heart' there are immediate associations and your awareness tends to drop to your breast area? Isn't it interesting that a word can have that effect? For some people, saying the word 'heart' might actually give rise to a kind of resistance and a strong impulse not to go there. Isn't that also rather interesting? This is the kind of thing that one gently explores as one trains in the discipline of meditation. One gradually discovers and lets go of layer upon layer of confusion as one recognizes what that resistance is about, and the heart becomes more free to open.

The importance of emphasizing the heart

Although we have strong intuitions about the heart, and many phrases in our culture that indicate its significance, you might be surprised at how much I am emphasizing it. I do this because I believe these intuitions and phrases point with astonishing accuracy to our true nature, right to the very essence of our being. It is as if we are sensing within us the awesome reality that in Buddhism is called the 'Awakened Heart'. Although we do not see it clearly, it is present within us as the ground of our being, unchanging and always awake. That is why it is called the 'Awakened Heart'. Even though we are not yet fully Awake, it is already complete and functions in our experience at every moment. For example, it is what makes us laugh and cry; it is what makes us feel alive and propels us ever onwards in search of happiness and the path of Awakening. It is present in us even in the midst of all our pain and confusion, our anger and desire, our host of fears and doubts.

Although I will be using the terms Awakened Heart, awareness, reality, and true nature, there are many terms for what I am talking about within the Buddhist tradition. For example, it may be referred to through its aspects of Openness, Clarity, and Sensitivity. At death or Enlightenment (Awakening), when is shines forth so vividly, it is called Clear Light Mind. It is called the Indestructible Heart Essence to emphasize its unchanging essence and that it is found in the heart as the core of our being. To emphasize its very nature being Buddha, with all the qualities of a Buddha, it is called Buddha Nature. Because to realize it means the end of suffering it is called Nirvāṇa. Because all things emerge from it, it is called the Primordial Ground.

When presenting the Buddha's teachings, it is important to stress heart at the outset so that everyone can understand we are talking about something meaningful and important. It suggests there is something of value to be discovered and understood. Unless those one is talking to already have faith that there is a meaningful reality to be discovered, it can sound nihilistic to start off talking about the inevitability of suffering and how all is impermanent and unreliable and ultimately unreal.

I mention this because the reader may be wondering why most traditional Buddhist teachers start by emphasizing these depressing sounding ideas, whereas I put more emphasis on what is unchanging, real, and of the highest value. This is because in traditional Buddhist cultures most people share the underlying assumption that Awakening or Enlightenment involves the realization of some great ineffable truth concerning the heart. The problem for teachers was not so much that their charges lacked faith in that reality (in the way that perhaps we do in western society) but that their attachment to the things of this life sapped their motivation to realize it as soon as possible. That is why their teachers tended to start by stressing the impermanence, unsatisfactoriness, and unreality of the things people were attached to.

But I find it is necessary to start by first giving those who come to me some sense of the Buddhist perspective on what is real and how that relates to what they intuitively value in their heart, so that they know there is something to hope for and aspire to. This can then be a motivation for reflecting on how impermanent, unsatisfactory, and unreal everything else is.

That might then motivate them to adopt the discipline of regular meditation practice in order to deepen their understanding of that initial intuition and inspiration concerning the nature of reality which they have found in their own hearts. What we all need to develop is a sense of an underlying trust in what is in our heart that can carry us through life and death. That is what takes the time and requires commitment.

Openness, Clarity, Sensitivity

You may be wondering how all this talk of heart and Awakened Heart relates to the fundamental unchanging awareness that I talked about in the previous chapter as being our true nature, the source of all the appearances of life and death. Actually, heart and awareness are just different ways of talking about fundamentally the same reality. It is an ungraspable reality in the sense that any idea we have of it is not it. It is beyond ideas. It is the reality that all ideas point to and emerge from. Its infinite qualities are ungraspable, too. The closest parallels in our own culture to this kind of vision seem to lie in places as diverse as ancient myths and modern physics, as well as the accounts of mystics from all the world's religious traditions.

In the Mahāmudrā and Dzogchen tradition of Tibetan Buddhism, this reality is spoken of in terms of three aspects, Openness, Clarity, and Sensitivity. The Openness is a sense of the vast unknown. It cannot be encompassed by thought; it is empty in the sense of there being nothing to hold on to; it is groundless. The Clarity is the knowing aspect of awareness, deeper than what we usually think of as knowing, in which all that we experience appears as though in a mirror. The Sensitivity is the responsive quality of awareness, the whole dimension of heart and meaning, pain and joy.

These three qualities are inseparable aspects of a single reality. For example, when we speak of an open heart, we are referring to all three aspects together; openness, clarity, and sensitivity are all implied. When we speak of life in any sense we mean the living essence that is aware and sensitive and yet ungraspable. Openness, clarity, and sensitivity are always present in all our experience.

Openness, clarity, and sensitivity are actually more familiar to us than anything else we can think of. Thinking itself is of exactly this nature. Look at the thoughts that appear in your mind. Are they something other than these three qualities? Even our confused emotions like anger, attachment, pride, jealousy, and despair are actually expressions of Openness, Clarity, and Sensitivity. Anger is ungraspable; you cannot pin it down as anything or being anywhere, yet it is sharply aware and intensely sensitive. It is the same for all our confused emotions. Isn't this amazing? Even in our worst moments, everything we experience is actually a manifestation of our true nature. There is no one who is separate from this reality.

When scientists search for the nature of awareness, they find nothing other than its manifestations. Subjectively and intuitively it is the arena in which things appear, but that arena is inaccessible to the investigating mind trying to pin down what awareness is. Thus, to that investigating mind, awareness is groundless and empty in the sense that it cannot be grasped as an object of awareness, much like an eye can see visible objects but not itself. Awareness knows objects that appear within it, but cannot take itself as an object in the same way. This makes awareness mysterious, but to itself there is no doubt about its presence, vivid, alive, and unmistakable. Awareness is primary. It is on the basis of the presence of awareness that we know anything at all. So life itself is life as we know it, and that is nothing other than the three indivisible qualities of openness, clarity, and sensitivity. These three qualities are mysterious but they are not something hidden. They are facets of all our immediate experience, whether we are thinking about them or not, whether we realize that is true or not, and whether we acknowledge them or not. None of us is different from this mysterious, ungraspable reality, aware and responsive.

Since the essence of all our experience is openness, clarity, and sensitivity, all direct experience is this ungraspable reality. For example, sweetness is an experience, but the essence of sweetness cannot be grasped. We don't actually know how to describe it. All we know is that it just is. That is its open, spacious, empty, ungraspable quality, but we only know it because it is manifesting clearly and precisely. It vividly manifests in our awareness, but we cannot in any way pin it down or define it. Ultimately, it is always that unknowable essence of any experience that gives it its deepest significance. That is what we are sensitive to and respond to.

It is important to understand that when we talk in Buddhism about seeing directly what we experience, or coming to understand our true nature, we are not talking about what we usually assume is knowing. Through meditation we come to realize our usual assumptions about knowing are false. We are talking about a way of knowing that has precision and clarity, but at the same time grasps no object. It is mysterious yet totally simple and in some sense ordinary. It is not hampered by the complications of the ordinary thinking process. To master it takes a long path of training.

Since openness, clarity, and sensitivity are fundamental to all experience, this must include what we call the heart itself. Isn't the heart potentially the most open, spacious and ungraspable, clear and aware, sensitive and responsive aspect of our experience? Even when we feel utterly depressed and miserable, an essential part of that experience is the sense of wrongness, a sense of 'it shouldn't be like this'. Isn't that complaint coming from the openness, clarity, and sensitivity of the heart itself?

Meditation is about gaining confidence in the openness, clarity, and sensitivity of our true nature. The openness, clarity, and sensitivity are our true nature and it is this true nature that is trustworthy. It doesn't change in life or in death. If we can learn to trust it, we will not feel so lost and helpless when death takes everything else away from us.

How the heart becomes confused

You may be wondering why, if we already have all these qualities, there is any need for meditation and a Buddhist path. The answer is that we have become confused. Although we have the Awakened Heart within us, we do not recognize it.

The good news is that because awareness and thus clarity is intrinsic to our nature, we have an inherent sense of truth, a power to distinguish what is true from what is false. The more we let go of our thoughts based on false assumptions about the nature of reality, and the more we trust ourselves to be open and simple, the more easily we can exercise that inherent power of clarity. Through it we discover that we have ceased to recognize, and therefore have lost confidence in, the true nature of our being. From this non-recognition, called *avidyā* in Sanskrit, which is often translated as ignorance, springs fear, which is what loss of confidence is all about. We turn away from our experience, our true nature, out of fear and try to dull it out. This is what perpetuates our confusion, our non-recognition and loss of confidence. Loss of confidence makes us grasp at what is not real as real, and causes us to be born and to die again and again.

The more we let go of what is not real, the more we open to our true nature. This allows an intuitive sense of truth to bubble up. As we learn to trust that, the more easily we recognize the falseness of our fears. So as well as confusion, we also have the clarity to recognize that it is confusion. The confusion is temporary and can be dispersed as darkness is dispersed by light. We learn to turn towards whatever we are experiencing and let go in this way, which means that everything in life and at death becomes the path to Awakening.

So the lack of trust in our intrinsic clarity and sense of truth causes us to identify with and become attached to what is not real as real. As we rely more on our inherent sense of truth, our clarity becomes stronger, so we are more likely to notice how we identify with our thoughts and feelings: how we cling to them as if to let go would be like death. Well, it is like death really. For example, if you are very angry and you were to say to yourself, 'just drop it,' part of you would feel, 'I can't drop it. Who would I be if I just dropped it?' Similarly, who would we be if we found ourselves lost in a dream and someone woke us up? We wouldn't be that person in the dream any more, that is for sure.

And when we die, we cease to be the person we were, and we wake into a whole new space. It is our clarity that wakes, but would we be able to let go of our attachment to the life that had gone? Meditation is for training in clarity, and also for training in letting go of attachment to that which is unreal.

You may be thinking that turning towards thoughts and feelings in life is one thing, but at death we really do lose our identity, when we lose our body and our connection with this world and this life. But you might become less sure of this when you start to explore what you really mean by your body and this life. One thing you might notice when you meditate is that you can't tell where thoughts are happening. We tend to say they happen in the head or the mind, but we don't know anything about the inside of our head directly. We only know we have a head because of a whole lot of ideas and memories that we put together. Awareness is not in the head, rather the head is an idea that is in awareness. In fact, we have no idea where awareness is! Mind, body, space, self, other, time, and so on, all turn out to be very mysterious. Our old ideas of what they are can get very shaky. We might even start to wonder what anything is at all.

The good thing about this is that it no longer seems so obvious to us what life and death mean. What is there to die that has not already slipped into the irretrievable past? Yet intuitively we sense that there must be more to what it is to be a person than a vanished event. Meditation is the process of discovering what that 'more' is. So, just like the Buddha, and all those who have followed the path to Awakening before us, as we go deeper, we inevitably have to start to question what we mean by 'me', where it came from, where it is now, and where it goes. By means of questioning and wondering and focusing again and again on our direct experience within the process of meditation, we discover the nature of our hidden assumptions that keep us stuck in a state of confusion. That is when we start to really wake up.

The traditional metaphor for this confusion is a layer of clouds that has hidden the sun of our true nature. Clouds are insubstantial, and in a sense they are nothing other than the sky itself. The clouds are not really anything, while the sun never changes. This is a partial image, but quite a good one in this context as it suggests a bursting forth of the brilliance of our true nature as we wake up and the clouds of our confusion concerning the world of the senses begin to disperse.

Not recognizing our true nature is like profound blindness. On top of the blindness accumulates layer upon layer of confusion, making our true nature extremely hard to recognize, and even harder to trust. In a sense, our true nature haunts us like some vast and unbearably brilliant splendour, too overwhelming for comfort. Part of us wants that brilliance, but part of us doesn't. It's too much. It is something we wouldn't mind experiencing for a moment or two, but then the tendency is to want the cosiness of our limited sense of self that we're familiar with. That is why we unconsciously dull out that vision.

That vast, open brilliance exposes the falsity of our confused sense of little me, so that little me interprets the experience as painful. The little me feels threatened by the brilliance because of fear of annihilation. In a sense, we are constantly driven by this fear of suffering and annihilation. We unconsciously try to suppress that fear by dulling it out. We dull it out from moment to moment, in order not to experience the full brilliance of our awareness. It is not that we do this deliberately, or that we are even aware we are doing it. We may long not to do this, especially when we think about how this dulling out keeps us in saṃsāra and causes us to miss the true meaning of life and death. However, it has become such a strong habit that it takes lifetimes of meditation to remove it.

Through meditation we learn to rely on our inner sense of truth to distinguish what is true from what is false, and so learn to appreciate our true nature rather than dulling it out. We know how to be honest, genuine, and truthful in this way. We don't actually need anyone to tell us this, but until someone points it out to us, we tend to overlook what is going on in our immediate experience. That is why we need to meditate and why we need someone to instruct us.

Trusting the Awakened Heart at death

Meditation is about becoming aware of the three qualities of the Awakened Heart in all our experience, recognizing their significance and learning to trust them as the unchanging true nature of our being. This nature can be relied on both in life and at death. It is always present. It is never not there. Even at death it will continue. We do not need to be afraid that it will be annihilated or destroyed.

We do not need to fear that we will be cut off from others and the rest of reality. Reality expresses itself through us. We can never be truly cut off and isolated. Our true nature doesn't come and go, it just is, and it is exactly the same in all of us. By just being honest and simple, trusting our inner being, we are naturally communicating with others, with the rest of reality. We can trust it in ourselves and trust it in others. When we open our hearts to each other, we sense this unchanging nature that we have in common, and somehow that satisfies the heart.

How do we know? How do we open our hearts to each other? How do we know what that means? We often call it intuition, but it is actually very precise direct knowledge. We open and we feel touched. That is all really. It's somehow too special and too deep to say much more about it.

Even those who never meditate can feel encouraged by merely the idea that there is such a path and that they have formed a living connection to it by being close to those who do. Because we all have the same nature, the connection between us all is very intimate, transcending all limits of time and space, self and other, and so on. So simply by opening our heart towards those who have a deeper understanding than ourselves, we form a connection to the path and that is able to help us find our way after death.

To not be connected to such a path is truly sad. On the other hand, a life connected to the path of Awakening is an increasingly meaningful adventure, in which each crisis teaches us how to relate to reality more appropriately. Death then becomes an opportunity for further practice.

THREE

The stages of death and rebirth

Buddhist teachings on death and rebirth tend to be presented either in terms of how things ultimately are, or in terms of how they appear to us in our deluded state.

In our deluded state it seems as if this world is real and we are really born here. At death we seem to leave as some kind of spirit that journeys into the strange, wild, unknown lands of the intermediate state and future births. Many Buddhists take this all quite literally, and many Buddhist teachings and practices are presented from this perspective, giving us guidance on how to ensure a good outcome on this journey.

In the earlier chapters of this book, I presented Buddhist teachings that offer a more profound perspective, describing how things ultimately are. I described how all the appearances of life and death actually take place in our awareness, so that in some sense we never go anywhere. Our confused existence is like a bad dream from which we could wake at any moment. These teachings are closely related to instructions on how to meditate, and reflect the understanding of our nature that naturally develops from extensive meditation practice.

Whichever of these perspectives they adopt, Buddhists in a traditional culture would also normally understand their path in the context of a vaster vision of the universe. They would know, from stories and background cultural messages, as well as from explicit teachings, that Awakened beings were there to help them, that our connections with other beings go from life to life, that our actions have karmic effects that rebound on us in future lives, and that already in our hearts lies the source of limitless goodness and meaning. This vaster vision is equally relevant, whichever of the two perspectives one adopts.

The difference is that meditators would be examining their experience as part of their quest to understand, eventually, for themselves what it all meant, rather than taking it all on board as a belief system and just trying to follow the instructions on how to get a good result. Westerners are often open and ready for the meditator's approach. Thus many, if not most, western Buddhists are more willing to begin their Buddhist practice by wrestling with the most profound teachings than by taking the literal-minded route that is traditionally regarded as easier.

This is why I have emphasized the profound meditator's perspective in the previous chapters of this book. Furthermore, giving careful consideration to the Buddhist cosmic view and its teachings on death does not mean that we have to adopt the whole package as a belief system. If we can at least remain open enough not to reject it all out of hand, and instead simply wonder and reflect on it, new possibilities of a deeper understanding might emerge. The reason we find certain ideas hard to accept is often that we are, consciously or unconsciously, making assumptions about the nature of the universe, time, space, self, and so on. Wondering about the Buddhist view helps us to notice such assumptions and allows us to question them. The effect of this can be to leave us less certain about our view of the world and more open to making new discoveries. This makes it easier, then, as the death process unfolds, for us to open out into it and respond to it appropriately.

In particular, we need to let go of the idea that the mind is some kind of by-product of the body. In Buddhism, mind or awareness is primary. The connection between the physical universe and the mind that appears to be born into it is profoundly mysterious. This is something we can explore in our direct experience at any moment. For example, we do not have the slightest clue which muscles we need to move in order to read this page, yet, by the mere intention to do so, we can do it. We have no idea how the minute patch of sensitive organic matter at the back of the retina translates into a screen on which images can play and deliver meaning. We have no idea what happens when that ceases to function. All we know is that the eye is dead and has ceased to function as an eye. But what happened to the screen? Where was it? Where is it? Can it function without an eye? We know it can. It functions in our dreams. There are many stories of how it functions at a distance where no physical contact is possible.

Some willingness to acknowledge the mysteriousness of our experience and its connection with the body is necessary to get much benefit from the more detailed Buddhist teachings on the stages of the process of dying and beyond, of which I give an outline in this chapter.

The basic stages of the process are:

- the dissolution process, which comprises the inner and outer dissolutions

- the actual moment of death

- the intermediate state after death

- rebirth

While there is a basic death process that happens to everyone, the exact sequence, timings, and how it is actually experienced, can all vary tremendously from person to person. It depends on a whole range of factors like the cause of death, one's state of mind, one's psychophysical constitution, one's past deeds (karma), and how well one is able to remember and practise what one has learned of the Dharma.

Nonetheless, it is useful to have some idea of the kind of things that might happen, much as it is useful to have some kind of map or guidebook when going on a journey. The terrain is the same, even if everyone experiences the journey differently. When you know the terrain you will be able to spot pitfalls ahead of time. From another point of view, since it's uncertain what exactly will happen, at least to have been forewarned of what is likely to unfold prepares one psychologically. You are less likely to be so shocked or to panic if you have some idea of what is likely to happen.

Sources and traditional texts

Although the Buddhist teachings expressed in this section (and elsewhere) are explained primarily from the point of view of the Dzogchen tradition, in principle they are in accord with Buddhist beliefs across most traditions. In other words, the same attitudes and the same kinds of customs are observed at the time of death by most Buddhist traditions.

Buddhist teachings on death and the dying process are based on three main sources:

- The teachings of people who have actually Awakened, who have gone beyond the confusion of birth and death. For example, the fundamental Buddhist scriptures attributed to the Buddha himself.

- The accounts of expert meditators who have direct experience of the process of dissolution in meditation that is paralleled by the death process. Their experience gives them an understanding of the mysterious connection between the body and the mind. They can in effect dissolve their body and mind into their timeless essence (the Awakened Heart), beyond birth and death, in this very life and body, and re-emerge from it as Enlightened or Awakened beings.

- The observation of and reports from advanced practitioners as they were actually dying. For example, it is said that Dodrupchen Rinpoche, a very accomplished Tibetan practitioner who died in the late eighteenth century, faced the end of his life in an amazing way. He did not appear to be ill, but simply sat in meditation, describing to his students the stages he was going through and his experiences as he died.

In the Tibetan Buddhist tradition there are various manuals explaining what happens during the process of dying, at the moment of death, and in the intermediate state before rebirth. In the West, the most famous of these manuals is the so-called *Tibetan Book of the Dead*, which has been available in English since the early twentieth century, and unfortunately subjected to some bizarre translations and misinterpretations.

Texts like the *Tibetan Book of the Dead* are very difficult to truly understand. For example, they make much use of terminology and images connected with the elaborate descriptions given in certain esoteric areas of Tibetan Buddhism about how the mind and body relate. But without understanding the fundamental ungraspability of mind or body, such descriptions can be very misleading. One might get the impression that one has to adopt some complicated intellectual theory about the subtle body, winds, and elements and how they correspond to various aspects of Enlightenment represented by different symbols and figures that might appear as described in these teachings.

When I read such descriptions out of context, I sometimes find all the different things to remember quite distracting and confusing. You have to decide for yourself whether this kind of teaching really helps you to link intuitively into your direct experience and give you confidence at the time of death, or whether they simply distract you from what you connect to most genuinely and naturally. It is possible that certain teachings could end up undermining your confidence simply because you cannot understand or connect with them properly.

That is why, in this book, I have kept to a minimum the kind of technical detail such manuals specialize in. Since most western Buddhists lack the doctrinal context of Tibetan Buddhism, these manuals can be quite confusing and unhelpful, even for experienced Buddhist practitioners. My aim, therefore, is to keep to the points that are relevant and helpful for more or less everyone when facing death. As Sogyal Rinpoche says,

> *The* Tibetan Book of the Dead *is destined for a practitioner or someone familiar with its teachings. For a modern reader it is extremely difficult to penetrate, and raises a lot of questions that simply cannot be answered without some knowledge of the tradition that gave birth to it. This is especially the case since the book cannot be fully understood and used without knowing the unwritten oral instructions that a master transmits to a disciple, and which are the key to its practice.* [*]

While preparing this book I made particular use of a text called *The Mirror of Mindfulness*, written in the seventeenth century by a very highly regarded Tibetan teacher called Tsele Natsok Rangdröl. This is a manual that draws on many other texts, such as *The Tibetan Book of the Dead*, and gives detailed explanations with sensible practical advice. It talks pragmatically about the things that can happen for different people, what is normal, and what is more unusual.

Two eminent lamas of the Nyingma tradition of Tibetan Buddhism in the twentieth century, His Holiness Dilgo Khyentse and Tulku Urgyen, both encouraged the translation of this text into English. Tulku Urgyen said (pp.1–2),

---

[*] Sogyal Rinpoche, *The Tibetan Book of Living and Dying*, Rider 2002, p.107.

The author of this text, Tsele Natsok Rangdröl, was an extremely learned and accomplished master of Tibet.... A great and eminent master, he fully comprehended all the teachings of the schools of Tibetan Buddhism, especially Kagyü and Nyingma.... A great number of explanations and commentaries on the bardo states exist. The text here is the most lucid and concise among them.... Tsele's writings are quite amazing.

Nonetheless, *The Mirror of Mindfulness* is still not easy to understand. It is written mainly for advanced practitioners and assumes familiarity with a huge array of Buddhist doctrines. That is why I feel the need to write this chapter, to communicate the important points more clearly.

I do not want to give the idea that there is no point to these other manuals. They could be very useful for an adept meditator who has a good experiential understanding of the Buddhist teaching on the true nature of reality, and who has already begun to master in meditation some of the stages of the subtle dissolution processes that occur at death.

For the rest of us, this broad outline is all we need. The technical details vary and tend to focus on subtle changes during the death process. However, when it comes to what one should do about these changes in practice, the instructions are the same regardless of the stage in the death process we have reached. In other words, the same instructions are applied to increasingly subtle experiences.

This means that it is enough just to remember the key instructions and apply them to the best of one's ability. Such instructions consist of simple reminders, such as to relax, let go, and trust the heart. They help give us the confidence to let the death process take care of itself.

One of the most important instructions is to turn towards whatever experience is coming up and just open to it, standing your ground, not shrinking away or trying to escape it, however frightening. The more we can do this, the more we can remain in touch with our basic sanity by just letting those appearances come and go, remaining centred and connected to our heart, whatever happens. Our heart is our connection with the true nature of our being, our connection with all beings, and in particular our connection with the Dharma and all Awakened beings. Simply being confident that this is the case will see us through all the experiences surrounding our death and what happens afterwards.

The dissolution process

Even though the fundamental nature of awareness never changes, it is obvious that something very significant is changing, both physically and mentally, as we die. In Tibetan Buddhism this is described as a process of dissolution. Before discussing this experience, I want to give a sense of the principles behind the process.

The teachings about the dissolution at death are based on teachings on the mind, body, and their relationship, which describe a whole structure of elements, *prāṇas* (winds), *nāḍīs* (channels), and *bindus* (essences) that are said to pervade and animate our body. According to Natsok Rangdröl, these gather in the heart during the dissolution process. What is this structure? Clearly it is not physical in the ordinary sense, since one does not find it when dissecting a body. Actually it is no other than Openness, Clarity, and Sensitivity, the true nature of awareness. This is animating our physical body and it is essentially this that moves within itself, withdrawing its display into the heart. In some mysterious way, our mind and our body and the world we live in emanate from the essence or true nature of the heart. Therefore what we think of as the physical heart is not the whole of what the heart really is. When the physical heart dies the essence of the heart (Openness, Clarity, Sensitivity) remains.

Once we die, others can still see and touch our body, but our mind is no longer in it. Some kind of disconnection has happened, even though we can still be aware of what is happening in the shared world that we are leaving. It is rather like pulling out a plug, so that electric current no longer animates the appliance. Subjectively, all this is experienced as something earth-shattering. One is aware that some kind of irreversible process has been set in motion and that one is being separated with some force and at some speed from all one knew in this life.

The process of dissolution is accompanied by a whole series of signs and stages, paralleled by what expert meditators experience in meditation. This is described in terms of drawing the *prāṇas* into the central channel and the heart centre. It is a process that doesn't necessarily lead to death, or to Awakening, even though it is characteristic of both processes.

What exactly happens during the dissolution process at death depends on many conditions. What is of most significance is our power to choose our attitude. Thus, if the dissolution occurs in a state of trusting the Awakened Heart and one's living connection with a lineage of practitioners dedicated to Awakening, it is easy to go to a rebirth favourable to continuing the path to Awakening. If the dissolution occurs in a state of strong attachment, anger, or fear, the outcome is less certain. Typically, if we are strongly egocentric at the time of dissolution, our tendency will be to panic and grasp at those aspects of oneself that are slipping away. This is not only terrifying in itself, it is exactly what gives rise to further fear and possibly anger.

If the process of dissolution, either in meditation or at death, is accompanied by insight, it can lead straight into perfect Awakening. Insight here means an accurate sense of the significance of what is happening. It is a deep kind of understanding of the true nature of our being.

The traditional teachings about the *prāṇa-nāḍī-bindu* structure and its dissolution tell us something about the mysteriousness of the connection between what we take to be our mind and body. However, these teachings are not something that can really be understood theoretically; you need the meditation experience for them to become something more than strange words.

The outer dissolution

The dissolution process occurs in two stages. The first is called the outer dissolution, and is described in terms of the dissolution of the elements: earth, water, fire, air, consciousness, and space. These elements are not quite the physical phenomena as we ordinarily think of them, but the subtle essence of physicality. These elements dissolve into the heart during the death process, leaving what we call the physical body as a corpse. Tibetan manuals on death contain a tremendous amount of detail about how each stage of the outer dissolution is experienced and the different signs that appear, as this can be useful to expert meditators. The main features are as follows.

The experience of earth dissolving is described as an intensification of the sense of weight, as if something heavy were pressing down on one. It leaves one feeling weak and wobbly. Water dissolving is experienced as an intensification of the sense of fluidity, being swept along by a flood or something like that. It leaves one feeling parched and shrivelled. Fire dissolving is experienced as an intensification of heat and a sense of burning, and leaves one feeling cold. Air dissolving is experienced as an intensification of a sense of movement, as if being blown about, and leaves us immobile.

In *The Mirror of Mindfulness* Natsok Rangdröl explains that when the subtle element of air dissolves, a breathing pattern of long exhalations and short rasping inhalations begins (presumably this is what in the West is called Cheyne-Stokes breathing). The eyes turn upwards, the mind feels bewildered, and one may see visions.

When the consciousness element dissolves, the heart and breathing stop, and the heat begins to leave the body, except for slight warmth around the heart. According to Natsok Rangdröl, even at this point the death process can be arrested and one can return to life.

The inner dissolution

The inner dissolution is more subtle, and occurs after our heart stops beating. We are at this point dead from a western medical perspective, though not yet so from a Buddhist point of view. What is dissolving in the inner dissolution is the thinking mind. This occurs in stages, first the gross and subtle thoughts of aversion, then attraction, and finally delusion. The subjective experience of this is described as white, red, and black lights, but the details of how exactly that takes place vary tremendously from one person to another.

The white light is usually experienced first, as thoughts of anger and hatred dissolve. It is accompanied by a feeling of great peace and contentment. It seems that the death process can still be arrested, in certain circumstances, even after the white light has started to appear, but not once the experience is complete.

Then there is an experience of the red light, as thoughts of desire and attachment dissolve. It is said that some people have fearful visions at this point, while some see scenes of welcome by messengers of Awakening from the Pure Lands. It is sometimes said that these visions occur earlier in the death process, in which case a return to life is possible even after they have started to appear.

The next experience is of the black light, as thoughts of delusion dissolve. This is not unconsciousness or blanking out, but a strange experience that can arise in meditation even in life. There is a sense that the whole world is dissolving. The person feels they are about to be totally annihilated. Most people are terrified by the black light. This is the point of the death process that is particularly associated with suffering. Some teachers say it is such a strong experience that, even in so-called peaceful deaths, it is a terrible suffering. But according to Natsok Rangdröl, in some people even this might be passed over in a state of general dullness. Once the black light has appeared there is no coming back. That is the final moment of life in that body.

How long do these stages of outer and inner dissolution last? Natsok Rangdröl says that 'most often the stages pass quickly'. In particular, he suggests that these three lights generally last only for an instant.

Although the stages of outer and inner dissolution are described in great detail in the texts, Natsok Rangdröl says there is a lot of variability from one person to another. For example, some stages may occur all at once in an almost momentary fashion, while other stages might last for what seems like ages. In fact, all the stages can happen instantaneously, as in a sudden or violent death. Also, dimmer versions of the lights can appear before the actual light experiences and may be dull, glittering, or smoky.

Since these experiences vary tremendously from one individual to another, it is best to prepare oneself for anything. The detailed descriptions are meant to give a general idea of what might happen in order to help one prepare oneself. So although for the expert meditator there are opportunities for insight in being able to recognize all these stages as they occur, for the rest of us they are not particularly relevant. In fact, trying to recognize the stages could be an unfortunate distraction.

The actual moment of death

When the outer and inner dissolutions are complete, our true nature is laid bare. In Tibetan Buddhist manuals on the death process, this is the moment that is described as the dawning of Clear Light, another term for our true nature. It shines forth because the non-recognition (*avidyā* or 'ignorance') that was obscuring it dissolves for a short time. Once this has happened, there is no way a person can return to their former life. From a Buddhist perspective, it is the actual moment of death.

This experience of severance is a tremendous wrench and a severe shock. Until now, the physical body has acted as a filter that has damped and narrowed things down; without it, the vividness, power, and intensity of unconstrained awareness is let loose. This is what we try to protect ourselves from when we cling to our sense of self in this life. We are trying to find a stable and secure place where we can hide and feel we are in control of things. In fact, there is no need, since all we are trying to run away from is the nature of our own being. Having failed to recognize it, we try to flee from it.

As the moment of severance approaches, the movement within awareness, which we identify as our self, which is constantly trying to grasp and secure itself, senses danger, so the tendency to grasp and panic intensifies. This is where it helps to have practised lots of meditation, since meditation is about turning to face our worst fears without grasping at them as real, without letting the emotion of fear drive us. We just let the experience of the fear be. The more we just let it be without feeding it, the more freedom of choice we have and the more confidence and trust we have in our basic sanity and heart. This is what helps us the most at that time and makes it easiest for others to help us.

This idea that all beings dissolve into the true nature of being at death is not common to all Buddhist traditions, so not all of them say that the time of death is an opportunity for resting in it and realizing liberation there and then. Having said this, in all Buddhist traditions it is recognized that something extraordinary occurs at the death of a Buddhist saint or adept. But even in the Mahāmudrā and Dzogchen tradition, where there is a lot of discussion of this point, it is understood that gaining liberation by dissolving into the true nature of being at death is the highest spiritual accomplishment, and that for most people the moment of dissolution is not noticed. Furthermore, even when it is recognized, the practitioner finds it hard to rest in it. That is why, normally, it is one's general attitude and habits of mind that are the most important determinants of what will happen next.

Subjectively, we may experience the sudden revelation of our true nature at the time of death (the Clear Light experience) as little more than a kind of shock. This is a sudden and very strong blanking out reaction, a turning away from the experience, that causes us to forget what happened and look back on it as simply having passed out. The first we really know of our having died might occur much later when we emerge from that period of blanking out. In other words, we might have passed through the Clear Light of the moment of death without realizing what was happening. We might have felt a sense of dread and rising panic, and passed out quite early in the dissolution process, so it is very hard to say what we might or might not have been aware of, or might remember afterwards. As explained earlier, the situation is similar to falling asleep. Because we are likely to have dulled out long before the Clear Light dawned, all we experience is waking up again, and all we remember when we look back is that we suddenly blanked out and were asleep. Objectively, the Clear Light experience is said to last for a certain period of time. This is usually just a moment, but it could be much longer in the case of a very advanced practitioner.

Near-death experiences

In recent years there has been much description of near-death experiences by a whole range of people who have come very close to death. Sometimes their hearts stopped beating but they could be resuscitated using medical technology. Generally, but not always, these experiences are felt as positive. Sometimes they are not only not particularly positive, but might involve terrifying visions. I suspect most people who have had bad experiences blank them out and don't report them.

Details of these accounts vary a lot, but basic themes occur in a significant portion. A white light is often mentioned, and a sense of peace, and the feeling of being welcomed. Some people have interpreted these experiences as accurate reflections of what really will happen at death. So they believe the experience of death and beyond will be painless, joyful, fearless, and lead easily to a pleasant outcome. From the Buddhist perspective, this might give them a false sense of confidence because, although they might feel confident in the initial stages of the death process, it is likely to be short-lived. As the full death process kicks in, they could have a terrible shock. They might not be prepared for the sense of utter annihilation associated with complete dissolution and the frightening experiences of the intermediate state. These experiences are all the more terrifying for being the complete opposite of what they expect.

So I feel it's important to stress that, from the Buddhist perspective, it is a sad mistake to take near-death experiences to reflect the full death experience. Near-death experiences are by definition not the death experience, since it is not possible to come back from the latter, whereas it is from the former. One cannot be sure that the one experience will accurate reflect the other. The experiences that people who have near-death experiences find so reassuring are in fact much more obviously equivalent to the earlier and less shocking stages of the process of dying than to the final death experience itself.

For example, the experience of a white light and a sense of peace might be the experience of the white light that happens as desire dissolves. The feeling of being welcomed seems to correspond to the visions that are traditionally said to occur at various points, particularly just before or after the white light. However, it is important not to confuse the white light of the near-death experiences with the sudden revelation of the true nature of reality (the so-called Clear Light) at the actual moment of death. Whereas, according to Buddhist tradition, someone can return to this life even after the white light appears, it is not possible to return once the Clear Light has dawned. So it would be wrong to confound the two experiences. A near-death experience is quite literally that. It is not the same as an actual death experience, and there is no reason to assume that, just because a near-death experience was not frightening, death itself will not be frightening.

The intermediate state

At some point after the sudden revelation of our true nature, our awareness starts to move again and our consciousness finally parts company with the body. The body is now a corpse. We then flit here and there (just as our consciousness does now), but since we are no longer restrained by our connection to the physical body, there is no longer a sense of basic confidence in an underlying stability and security as there was in life. However, just as in a dream, we feel we still have a body and can engage with whatever is appearing. This is the intermediate state (*bardo*) between death and rebirth. The being wandering in this state is called a *gandharva* (which is more or less what in English would be called a spirit of some kind).

The commentarial tradition of Theravāda Buddhism does not talk of an intermediate state as such. Nevertheless, the consciousness is thought to leave this body and find its way to another body in some way or other in a form called a *gandharva*. In principle, this does not sound that different from what Tibetans call the *gandharva*-being in the intermediate state. It is just that the Tibetan tradition seems to go into much more detail.

Taken literally, a *gandharva* in the intermediate state sounds like some kind of little entity hopping from one life to the next. But from a deeper perspective, it is nothing other than the essence of what we are as a person, distorted by a mistaken idea of itself (just as in life). This distorted or false idea of what it is causes the *gandharva* to cling to what is not its body as its body (much as we do in dreams) and takes its own projections as real (as we do all the time in life). But until it has taken birth in a stable world, it can change worlds, bodies, and mind states at terrifying speed.

Since, when we awaken in the intermediate state, we are unlikely to remember what has happened, we might easily believe we are still alive in our old body. Proceeding to act as normal, we might get up and feel fine, but notice that our friends and relatives were acting strangely. So we might feel angry seeing, for example, other people handling our possessions. This would be very dangerous, and propel us towards states of intense suffering. Furthermore, it is said that in this state we know what others are thinking. For this reason, it is helpful for the living to talk to the dead, either out loud or mentally, explaining what has happened and why one is doing what one is doing, reassuring the deceased person and giving them advice, such as not to be afraid or angry.

This is because without the physical body to restrain it, every movement of the consciousness of the *gandharva* causes its whole world of experience to change very quickly and dramatically. This means that a negative emotion, such as anger, can immediately propel it into a fearful, hellish state. Gendun Rinpoche (one of my teachers) once compared this to taking a wrong turning off a highway; very quickly one finds oneself way off course. Kind and generous thoughts at that time are much more powerful, so if you can recall the Buddha, Dharma, and Sangha, your meditation, or any other spiritual practices at that time, it helps tremendously. If you are well trained in meditation, as the fear caused by the instability and frightening apparitions arises, you can use that fear as a trigger for awareness: turn towards that fear, and let it go. The fear arises through not recognizing that what appears is nothing other than the display within the space of our own awareness. The temptation is to try to run from what is appearing. Don't run! There is nothing to run from. If you run it will seem as though you are being pursued. If you turn towards the fear, you might remember that the openness, spaciousness, emptiness of awareness that is always our nature never changes. Recalling your practice in this life, you will be able to trust in that experience. That trust is in itself an expression of our sensitivity, responsiveness, and sense of well-being. The awareness that can turn towards experience and recognize it as its own display is the clarity aspect. These three aspects of the true nature of our being are always present and accessible at any stage of the death and rebirth process.

Although it can be terrifying, the intermediate state also presents special opportunities to make significant progress on the path, because the body is no longer holding us back. As soon as we think of the path of Awakening, it is very easy to practise because at that moment the path becomes our whole world. As soon as we think of Awakened beings, we are in their presence.

Best of all would be to have deep insight into our true nature, but if we remember even one word of Dharma, it can have a huge effect. Natsok Rangdröl quotes (p.83) from an authoritative text:

> *One may wonder why it is that one can attain stability merely by recognizing one's nature for one instant at the time of the bardo. The reply is that at present the mind is encased in the net of the wind of karma, the wind of karma is encased in the net of the material body of flesh and blood, and therefore one has no independence. After this body has separated into matter and mind, the prāṇa-mind, along with its magical displays, has no concrete material support during the period in which one has not yet become encased in the net of the future body.... One's capacity to attain stability by merely recognizing is like a torch which in one instant can clear away the darkness of aeons. If one has recognition in the bardo just as one now has when receiving the pointing-out instruction, then there is no doubt about attaining enlightenment. Therefore, from this very moment make yourself acquainted.*

So at any moment in the intermediate state, on recollecting our practice and our connection to the path of Awakening, we can be liberated very quickly. It is important to make this point because there is so much emphasis, in certain traditional teachings, on 'getting it right' and not missing the crucial moment that they can sound scary and discouraging. However, examining these teachings more closely, you'll notice that even if you miss the moment of an important opportunity, there are still plenty of other opportunities. There is never any need to give up hope and think it's too late to practise.

In the Tibetan tradition this intermediate state is generally described as lasting forty-nine days. *The Tibetan Book of the Dead* and similar manuals go on to give quite detailed descriptions of this time. I will not go into that in detail, because I want to maintain attention on the essential points. The truth seems to be that the intermediate state is incredibly unstable and everything varies tremendously from person to person so that just about anything could happen. We need to know just enough to prepare ourselves to face our death and to help others face theirs with confidence.

Furthermore, more detailed manuals, such as that of Natsok Rangdröl, state that each of these forty-nine days of the intermediate state could pass in a flash or last a long time. So although the formal descriptions tend to make the process sound quite straightforward and fixed, it is not as neat and sewn up as it sounds. Even though the Tibetan funeral customs for giving spiritual help to the *gandharva* last forty-nine days, this figure is only a rough and ready one to help those dealing with the practicalities. For the departed consciousness, the experience of time is no longer related to this world. When we first enter the intermediate state, our awareness can remain somewhat connected to the world. But this becomes less and less the case as we start to move towards the world into which we are about to be born. It is uncertain how long all this will take. The *gandharva* might take off to another world very rapidly or hang around this one indefinitely.

We eventually see visions that present us with various options or gateways into stable worlds, even though it might not be obvious to us that this is what is happening. For example, in the case of a human birth we might have a vision of a palace, house, or cave where we feel safe, which means we are about to enter a womb. Although there are lots of tips given about how to recognize a gateway into human birth, I don't think that it is necessary to worry about this. Generally speaking, the chief determining factors at this point will be our past deeds (karma), our habits of mind, our intentions (past and present), and our connection to the path of Awakening. My advice is to rely on these rather than fill one's head with notions and fruitless speculations.

The death of advanced practitioners

From the Buddhist perspective, the death process is viewed as a particularly good opportunity for expert meditators to gain insight and even complete liberation from saṃsāra. It is an opportunity to Awaken, to gain liberation, which means it is an opportunity to cut through the cycle of birth and death by recognizing the true nature of reality and becoming one with it. One emerges from that state as an Awakened being.

This opportunity arises because those who train sufficiently during this life can take advantage of the brief moment when everything dissolves into the Clear Light and recognize it for what it is. This is called the child Clear Light meeting the mother Clear Light. This is done through the ability to recognize and rest in the Awakened Heart, and through the power (adhiṣṭhāna) of those who are already Awakened. For a really advanced practitioner, the experience of death might not even be a big deal because they would be used to recognizing the Clear Light nature as the basis of all their experience in life, so death is a variation of something familiar, rather than a new revelation. Even if an advanced practitioner cannot remain in meditation through the whole death process, he or she may still be able to make tremendous progress on the path at this time.

Very advanced practitioners might remain in the body in this state of meditation (called *samādhi* or *thukdam*) for some time (hours, days, or weeks). If such a practitioner has students who have faith in them, this can be a time of great intimacy in which profound transmission can occur, because the physical body is no longer in the way. The sign that the meditation has ended is that the heart area cools, the body fluids are released, and rigor mortis sets in. In general, it is thought best to leave the body undisturbed up to this point, so as not to interrupt the meditation. However, it is common to perform some gentle handling, for example sitting the body upright in meditation posture, or touching the heart area to see if it has cooled. An interruption to the meditation will not be a problem from the point of view of the advanced practitioner, but it would end this time of special opportunity for the students.

Even if the very advanced practitioner does not manage to fully recognize their nature at the moment of death, there are other special opportunities for them during the intermediate state. For example, there are special subtle appearances (inconceivable lights, sounds, and beings) that an advanced practitioner can recognize and make use of right at the beginning of the intermediate state (what is technically called the 'bardo of *dharmatā*'). Tibetan manuals on the intermediate states, such as *The Tibetan Book of the Dead*, contain detailed descriptions of this kind of thing because they can be of use to advanced practitioners. However, for most of us a simpler and safer option is to keep remembering our meditation practice and what we have most confidence in, and rely on that to pull us through whatever experience arises. Anyway, Natsok Rangdröl says that for ordinary beings these appearances will generally last only an instant. Quite possibly we will not even notice them.

Facing fear

Generally, fear is such an overwhelming aspect of the death experience that confidence, its opposite, is the most effective quality with which to face it. It could be said that essentially the whole Buddhist path, the whole path of Awakening, is about confidence. Confidence allows us to relax and let go of doubts and confusion, and it enables us to face our true nature without fear.

Fear characterizes every stage of the death process. There is the fear of leaving this familiar world, of losing everything we know, and being uncertain what will happen. There is the fear of pain and suffering in the death process. There is the fear of losing control as the death process takes over. There is the sense of impending doom as one faces the prospect of annihilation. There is fear of not being able to find one's way through the changes and visions in the intermediate states, and possibly even a fear of one's past deeds catching up with one. There is the fear of loneliness and abandonment, the fear of losing one's mind, and the fear of being so overwhelmed by the experience that one panics. In fact we can be more afraid of fear than of what we are actually afraid of. Since some or all of these fears are likely, we need as much courage as we can muster. It is vital not to panic but simply to turn towards the sensation of the fear itself and not react to it.

People shy away from even thinking about death because they somehow intuit that all these fears are there and they do not want to face the thought of annihilation. However, for those of us who want to follow the path to Awakening, death presents itself as a profound opportunity to further our practice. Rather than shy away from even thinking about it, we reflect on it as inspiration. It inspires our life as we try to live as we hope to die, and it helps us anticipate death with confidence as we move towards it in the same way that we have become accustomed to live. If we can maintain an underlying confidence, regardless even of intense fearful reactions, we learn that fear is not something to run from.

Tibetan teachings about death reiterate again and again that we just have to recognize whatever appears as being awareness itself, and there is nothing to fear. Natsok Rangdröl says (p.74)

One must in all situations resolve that the terrifying experiences that take place, no matter of what type, are the self-display of one's own mind.

How do we do that? Just as we do in our practice here in this life. How much of the time are we able to do this in our life now? Not much? Only on good days? Or, more likely, for a fraction of a second when we listen to a teaching or look deeply into the nature of our experience. In that case, we might as well forget the idea of being able to meditate through the violent upheavals of death and the states that follow. Even in the midst of fear, however, it is possible simply not to mind it and to remain centred and confident. The fear comes and goes. Our sanity remains. In the end we always come back to our basic sanity. It is indestructible. The more we relax, the sooner we return to it. That is true both in life and in death.

The many worlds of rebirth

All schools of Buddhism teach that once the death process is complete, the *gandharva* is driven to seek rebirth in some world or other. The driving force is karma, our previous volitional actions. So Buddhist teachings on death constantly allude to a worldview that takes for granted the existence of karma and many worlds. In the remainder of this chapter I give an overview of these ideas that makes them easier for a western reader to understand.

When the Buddhist teachings talk about rebirth, they are referring to it in the context of an infinite variety of worlds, not just different experiences of planet Earth (or even this physical universe). I have already talked in some detail about the many 'worlds' that appear in our awareness and which we enter and engage with. We have plenty of experience of being lost in such worlds created by our thought while we are awake and as dreams when we sleep. I have mentioned that, from the Buddhist point of view, getting lost in such thought-worlds is comparable with actual birth and death. What distinguishes birth from thoughts and dreams is that our births take place in shared worlds. They are not worlds that are just our own imagination or creation. The Buddhist view is that an incredible variety of worlds can appear in our awareness after death as potential birthplaces.

What is more, these worlds involve experiences far beyond what we can imagine. From the Buddhist perspective, our physical brain and sense organs are not, as materialists would have us think, the basis of consciousness. It is not the brain and sense organs that give rise to consciousness. Consciousness is aware-ness, and awareness is capable of experiencing everything that we experience through the brain and senses, without reference to the sense organs. If anything, our sense organs limit our awareness, rather than give rise to it. In other words, our body with its brain and five sense organs limits our experience to what they are capable of sensing. From the Buddhist perspective, the range of potential experience is limitless. For example, un-imaginable extremes of suffering and pleasure are possible. We could take birth in worlds characterized by either of these extremes and all manner of combinations in between.

Buddhist cosmology often presents these possibilities as six main classes of beings, the highest of which are various god realms where pleasure becomes increasingly rarefied and long-lasting, and the lowest of which are the various hell realms where suffering becomes increasingly intense and long-lasting. Neither heavens nor hells last forever. They eventually end and the cycle of birth and death continues. So even rebirth in a god realm is not regarded as desirable, because of the danger that its blissfulness would be so intense and enduring that we would lose our motivation to follow the path to Awakening. When we die in the god realm, we regard our imminent fall with dismay. The suffering of the fall of the gods is notorious. Having fallen, without insight into the true nature of reality, or a connection to the path of Awakening, we will simply be lost once again in the cycle of birth and death, never knowing where we are next going to have to suffer and die.

The important point to understand is that in the Buddhist view our predicament is very serious and our future very uncertain. Without a strong connection with the path of Awakening, we could end up anywhere. Since death can come at any time, the possible destinations are infinite. The Buddhist teachings make it clear that the kind of life we enjoy at present, in which we have the option to follow the path of Awakening, is a rare occurrence. It is hard to come by, and it is easily lost. But once we have made a strong connection to the path to Awakening, it is as if we have been hooked by a line that can pull us right out of that ocean of suffering by keeping us to the path from one life to the next. All we have to do is co-operate. That is what following the path to Awakening is essentially all about.

How karma shapes rebirth

We are talking here of a cosmos in which there are connections that span worlds and time. The effects of our actions and our wishes do not end here. They can ripen in times and places that have nothing to do with what we think of as this world and this life. In this sense our connections go with us and are more real than the world we are leaving behind.

The standard Buddhist teaching is that our volitional actions (karma) in this life determine what happens to us in future lives. This means that we find ourselves being born in worlds that we take to be as real as this one, reaping the fruits of our actions, good and bad. The fact that from the Buddhist perspective none of this is real doesn't help, because in terms of how things appear to us in our confused state, it is all real.

Karma means that if, for example, we act from love and kindness in this life, this will bring us happiness in future lives. Similarly, if we act from anger and hatred, it will bring us misery. This teaching on karma is not only saying that our current attitudes will affect our psychological attitudes in future lives, for example whether or not we will suffer when we get injured. It is more radical than that, in that it teaches that even some seemingly physical issues like what kind of body we have, or whether a certain injury will befall us, are also determined by our past volitional actions.

The Buddhist tradition goes into the causes and effects of karma in great detail, spelling out its implications in the context of countless beings spending countless lives wandering the countless universes that make up saṃsāra. It depicts each one of us having taken birth as every possible kind of being you can imagine (or not) over countless lifetimes, relating to each and every being in countless ways in every possible relationship, such as mother, child, friend, enemy, prey, predator, lover, sibling, king, servant, and so on. We have all been acting in every kind of way, accumulating a vast backlog of potential karmic results. Furthermore, we none of us know what is in the pipeline in terms of karmic results, or when they are likely to come to fruition. For example, something that happens to us today could be traced back to something we did many lifetimes ago in another world altogether. So the whole situation is very precarious.

From the Buddhist perspective, the uncertainty of karma is obvious from just looking at what is happening in the world around us. For example, good people suffer horrific illnesses, bad people seem to get away with murder. People are suddenly cut down in their prime, losing their wealth and health, family, friends, freedom, country, or whatever. We are never safe. We never know whether by the end of the day our whole life or world might not be changed. Even though it is taught that karma is driving all this, we are none the wiser about what might happen next. That is why Buddhism stresses the need to keep connected to the path to Awakening. The message is that karma and rebirth is like a nightmare and we need a path to Awakening so that we can awaken from it.

How helpful is the idea of karma?

In my experience, many western Buddhists do not really take on board the scale and extent of the cosmology of which karma is a part. They take on a few aspects of karma and stop there. This leads to a distorted view of the whole conceptual framework within which the teaching operates. Furthermore, westerners seem ready enough to believe that their negative actions will bring suffering, but are wary of believing too strongly that their good actions will bring them happiness.

It is for these reasons that in this book I do not talk in terms of karma as much as a traditional Buddhist book on the subject of death. Instead, I stress direct experience and trust, which are actually more fundamental in terms of what is necessary for the path of Awakening.

I do not do this because I am calling the Buddhist teachings on karma into question, but rather because the traditional teachings on karma assume a context that is not in place in the West these days. For example, many people say they don't want to believe in karma because they don't want to believe that those who are suffering are more at fault than those who are not. It feels cruel within the western context to say that the starving millions are in that situation because of their karma, implying that somehow they deserve it and I, the speaker, do not. Personally, I am really glad people don't like that idea! It is insidious.

As I said above, the Buddhist view is a more general sense that our lives are always precarious and what is happening to others today could be happening to us tomorrow. This is possible because we have all had countless lives in which we have probably done everything one could possibly think of, and none of us knows what karmic action will ripen next; in other words we are all in the same predicament of not knowing what awaits us.

I hesitate to stress this kind of teaching too much, because I find most westerners do not have a strong belief in the saving power of Awakened beings and their own connection with the path of Awakening, or anything else for that matter. So I look for things that will strengthen whatever faith they have, rather than stressing just how terrifying the cycle of birth and death really is.

If a person has a lot of trust in the Dharma and Awakened beings, and is open to the traditional Buddhist teachings on the nature of the cycle of birth and death and the uncertainty of what will happen next, then the most helpful thing of all can be to stress that. It reminds a person of their predicament in a way that galvanizes them to take action, to respond appropriately. However, it is no use talking in terms of karma to someone who is just going to get upset and full of doubts, especially since it is not absolutely necessary to think in those terms in order to follow the path to Awakening.

In order to keep to the path of Awakening you only need to keep to your direct experience and an emerging sense of trust. By simply relaxing and opening one's heart, one is making all the right karmic moves, even without having taken on board the worldview implied by karma.

We shouldn't forget that, ultimately, even the idea of karma is untrue. The standard account of karma does not really address the mystery of what a person is, and how we can each have our own karma. If Buddhism teaches that we are not little entities that hop from one life to the next with a bundle of karma tied to our backs, what carries the karma from life to life? How can what I do here in this world affect the shape and events of another world altogether? Such questions are not easily answered, because karma is a provisional truth that is only helpful when we are caught up in confusion.

It is not ultimately true, even though it can be helpful as a means of getting out of the confusion. It is helpful because it points to something real, which is that there is a real connection between our volitions, our actions, and our suffering. But the idea of karma does this rather crudely. It works very well in the same way as it works well to say the sun rises in the east. From a fundamental perspective the sun doesn't do any such thing. If someone had trouble believing it did, we would not have to insist they take on that belief. The important thing is that they relate appropriately to their experience.

Karmic debt

Traditionally, in Buddhist cultures where people have a strong belief in karma and past and future lives, practitioners often feel a sense of being burdened by the negative karma they believe they have accumulated in past lives. They think of this in terms of a karmic debt that traps them in saṃsāra and prevents their quickly traversing the path to Awakening.

Rather than feel burdened by a karmic debt in this way, western Buddhists tend to focus on the Buddhist teachings about being trapped in their habitual tendencies and driven by a distorted view of reality. This is no doubt because these are things that we know from our personal experience, whereas the idea of a karmic debt depends on our adopting a whole system of Buddhist beliefs. In general, I have found this is a significant difference between eastern and most western Buddhists. In the West we find it relatively easy to think in terms of the more distorted our view of reality gets, the more the burden of karma enmeshes us and makes it hard for us to escape. The traditional idea that somehow our karmic debt could be altered or purified is not one we tend to pick up on or find easy to relate to.

For example, one traditional way the burden is lessened is by suffering the consequences of something we have done and so, in a sense, complete the karmic sequence. The result of that karmic deed is then no longer waiting somewhere to come to fruition. So it is like having paid off a debt.

To talk in terms of a debt is, of course, only a manner of speaking, but it fits the situation quite well. If you owe someone money, you are weighed down by that debt. Once it is paid you are free. Paying off a karmic debt feels like that. I have noticed that Tibetans can feel very cheerful in the face of great difficulty and suffering by considering this thought alone. They even thank the Buddhas for their blessing (*adhiṣṭhāna*) that made all this karma ripen at once, when they are able to practise Dharma and finish it all off. If they had died with that great debt, they might not have had such good conditions for finishing it off in a future life. So, traditionally, Buddhist practitioners welcome suffering as a way to pay off as much karmic debt as possible before they die.

The point here is that the karma is not so much a result of an action as a configuration that was set up at the time of the action, which is then somehow (in a timeless way) present as a trap we could fall into and suffer as a consequence. If we meet that configuration when we are securely on the path to Awakening, it is merely something we have to work with, in the sense of using it to develop patience or humility or whatever. It doesn't have to overwhelm us or lead us astray. Unfortunately, westerners sometimes understand these ideas to mean that suffering itself is inherently good, or something we have to endure because we deserve it. But this is not at all the point. It is just that living through such an event in a positive state of mind purifies it (so to speak), so that it is no longer the trap that it was.

The good news is that we do not have to relive all the possible configurations lying in wait for us in order to arrive at Awakening. Since they are infinite, that would be impossible. Although the configurations themselves are timeless, from our point of view they are occurring in time as if through a pipeline. There may be certain karmic configurations about to come up that can interrupt our path to Awakening if they catch us unawares. If they were to manifest in some form now, in this life, we could somehow pass through them while in a positive situation. The karmic configuration typically takes the form of an illness or some kind of loss or difficult situation which, if we accept it patiently, prevents that karmic configuration recurring before we are Awakened.

Awakened beings can sometimes alter the order in which actions ripen. So, for example, the effect of a bad action can be postponed either to such a far off time that we will be Awakened before its time comes, or at least to a time and place in which we will have maximum help in dealing with the consequences. By suffering a relatively minor problem now we can sometimes avoid having to suffer the full consequences of an action later. Ideas like these inform numerous Buddhist customs, rituals, and *praṇidhānas* within all Buddhist traditions, but little attempt is made to try to explain them.

Although this explanation offers a sense of the kind of thinking that lies behind the teachings on karma, it is of necessity incomplete and unsatisfactory. The Buddhist tradition is aware of this, but sees no way out of the problem, since how karma works is very mysterious (hidden). It can only really be understood by Buddhas themselves, when they come to understand the whole of the nature of reality. The essence of that reality, our true nature, is relatively easy to realize compared with such mysterious aspects as karma, which are much harder to discern. Nonetheless, we can grasp a rough idea of how this works in principle, which does for most practical purposes. It is like knowing how a telephone or computer works in the sense of knowing how to use them. We might not have a clue about the inner workings of such gadgets and for most practical purposes we don't have to.

This world-view, with its countless worlds and different forms of rebirth, lies behind all the Buddhist beliefs, customs, and practices at the time of death and sets the scene for the rest of this book.

FOUR

Trusting the heart

Since death comes without warning and often in circumstances of intense worry and uncertainty, it is easy to feel overwhelmed by the various emotions. With all the disruption and upset, all the difficult decisions, the waiting around and the tears, it's hard to stay calm and collected. But even if you feel overwhelmed, the fundamental attitude you bring to the situation can help you find your way through. From the Buddhist perspective, your attitude is what is most helpful and powerful during the process of death and afterwards. So in this chapter I will elaborate on what attitudes might be helpful. By 'attitude' I mean the whole orientation of our way of being. I do not mean we should simply adopt a psychological trick or stance, but that we link into a kind of opening movement in our awareness that gives us access to our own power and resourcefulness as well as to communication and strength from the universe in general and the world of Awakening in particular.

In other words, our attitude has real power in its own right. For example, when our attitude is one of trusting the heart – our connection to the fundamental nature of reality – this is not just a matter of grasping at an idea, it links into a power that is alive within us. It has its own resourcefulness. Our problem is that we tend to get in our own way, so to speak, by trying to control things and make things happen in a particular way. When our attitude is one of trust and not panicking, rather than feeling overwhelmed by events, we find we are naturally connected to our basic sanity, so that help and inspiration come to us. When, to take another example, our attitude is more concerned with the welfare of others than ourselves, this links into that same spontaneous resourcefulness of our being. Courage, fortitude, and wisdom flow naturally into us and take us over without our even having to think about it.

On the other hand, when our attitude is not trusting and relaxed, our inner resources are made inaccessible by tension and fear, and consumed by paranoia and worry. In that state, we are unable to make much use of any help that is offered.

Attitudes are cultivated throughout the course of one's life, and that is why it is the way that one lives one's life that chiefly determines what happens during the death process and thereafter. However, the attitudes I describe here are available to all of us at any point. The simple fact that a person can understand something of what I mean when I talk about 'trusting the heart' or 'relaxing' shows that they have some genuine connection with what I am referring to.

My message here is that an open attitude allows some kind of power or strength to come to us – and that is as true in death as it is in life. From the Buddhist perspective, this is because Awakening and confusion are simply a matter of how one sees, thinks, or apprehends reality. You could say that Awakening itself is nothing other than a fundamental change of attitude. This would explain why an attitude of openness and fearlessness at the time of death connects us strongly to reality. Having made this shift, reality with all its boundless resourcefulness could take us over. It has power from its own side. It doesn't need manipulating or controlling by our egocentric efforts. That is why the more we adopt an attitude of opening and aligning ourselves with reality, the less we have to actually 'do' from our own side.

In *The Mirror of Mindfulness* (pp.78–9) Natsok Rangdröl gives the traditional Buddhist teaching about the attitude to adopt towards one's death.

> *For best results, [be] delighted to die; second best, [be] without fear; or at least free from regret. This is the instruction of the most essential point.*

It is a sign of accomplishment to be able to face one's death with an attitude of confidence and joy. This is not the attitude of a person who is just laughing and joking and pretending nothing is happening, but the confidence and joy (which might indeed be accompanied by laughter) that comes from deep realization and confidence in the nature of reality. For those of us who fall short of this, we can at least hope to face death satisfied that we have lived our lives to the best of our ability. 'Free from regret' does not mean we are pretending to ourselves that we have led a perfect life. It means we have been honest and sincere in our repentance of wrongdoing, and feel confident and joyful about what we have done right. The regret referred to is that of realizing too late that one should have prepared for death ahead of time and taken more care in the way one has lived one's life. However, even if we do arrive at death with regret, it is not too late to have a change of heart. From the Buddhist perspective, this means there is no need to die despondent, because one would be galvanized and full of determination to act well in future. Thus, although we might not quite be fearless in the way Natsok Rangdröl means, we can still have a kind of underlying confidence and, as Natsok Rangdröl implies, this is the most essential point.

There are two different ways of understanding 'right' attitude here. On the one hand is the attitude of a deeply realized person or experienced meditator who knows how to rest in the Awakened Heart. On the other hand, there is the attitude or cluster of attitudes that anyone can have, even if they are not meditators or have no religious inclination.

The kind of attitudes I am thinking of are those we need to foster anyway in order to help us day by day. Exactly the same attitudes are essential in order to keep us on the path to Awakening. We all have the means to cultivate the kind of attitudes that we and others need when faced with death, and we can encourage them in others, Buddhist or not, following any spiritual path or none.

I am talking about an attitude of openness, clarity, and sensitivity, and all the nuances of those terms. In practice they manifest as kindness, generosity, acceptance, courage, patience, honesty, staying connected to one's heart, letting go of attachment, hopefulness, resolve, faith, equanimity, and so on. In openness, clarity, and sensitivity is found the power to link into our good heart connections with others. Simply to maintain and foster any of these attitudes of openness, clarity, and sensitivity is to practise Dharma at the time of death. You do not need to do anything more elaborate than this. If we do undertake more elaborate practices, they are only in order to foster and deepen the right attitude. It is the right attitude that does the work. An elaborate practice can be made counter-productive and a spontaneous gesture can be deeply significant, all depending on one's attitude.

It is our attitude to our own death that is going to carry us through dying and into our next life, it is also what is going to come across when we relate to others who are faced with death. It is because our underlying attitude will be so important that we need to reflect on the fact of death again and again, so that we come to it somewhat prepared.

Heart wish

To access our ever-present inner resources we need to connect to what I call the heart wish, a place within us that is the source of all our wishes. When I say heart wish, I don't mean some *thing* that we wish for; it's not our idea about what we think we would like, but a deep place in our being from which those ideas emanate.

When we ask ourselves what we want, it is as if there is a place within us where we go to look for the answer. What is that place that we direct the questions to? As answers come up, we return to that place to double-check that this is indeed what would satisfy our wish. We can then ask ourselves if we really want this or that, right in the depths of our hearts. In my experience, the question invariably means something. People's attention drops down into the chest area and, from somewhere at the heart of our being, answers seem to bubble up. In fact, it is as if the answer is already there and we are trying to articulate something we have sensed as a living presence or experience.

For example, you might say you want a new car, but when you ask why, and whether this is what you really want in your heart of hearts, you tend to focus on the heart area and feel something there. As you articulate that, it might come out with the words 'because it would be such fun,' as if somehow the whole thing were emanating from that wish. You might make a few more tries at the question and get answers such as, 'because I want to impress my friends'. Then, if you ask why, it is because you want to feel confident, and, if you ask why again, it is because you want to feel happy.

That is where it ends. You want to feel happy because you want to feel happy. Wanting to be happy is always there in our heart. It is our heart wish, the source of all our wishes.

When you think about it, there is something very interesting about that. It is as if the wish for happiness was there before you articulated it and it remains there to tell you whether the articulation is right or not. But what is that source of both the question and the answer? I am calling it the heart wish.

So the heart wish is not an articulated wish; it exists even without it ever being articulated. It is just there. When we really home in on what it is, it somehow seems to go deeper and deeper and perhaps even vaster and vaster. At first, we may find we just want a little physical comfort. But, if we look deeper, we may find we actually just want to feel free of a general sense of a lack of ease, and if we look deeper still, we might find that what we really want is to feel a sense of meaning, and if we look at that more deeply, we may find that what it is really about is wanting a sense of rightness and perhaps happiness, though actually it is something that goes beyond what we ordinarily call happiness. Or we may end up feeling a great longing to love and be loved, or a great longing for some revelation that will somehow make everything right.

However one formulates the wish, that place we go to look for it is right there. We know how to go there and how to ask it about our wish. It is inherent in our nature. That is the heart wish.

Sometimes I talk about our deepest heart wish because what happens eventually is that we come up with some kind of formulation that expresses a wish for our own happiness and the happiness of all other beings. If we explore long enough, we seem to come to this at the rock bottom. Sometimes it is deeply buried. Sometimes we think we don't really care about others or at least not all others. But when we keep going with this exploration, we end up realizing that we hate to suffer and we only want others to suffer as long as we suffer ourselves. Once we no longer suffer, it is horrible to have others suffer around us. We would naturally rather not have anyone suffer. So, deep down, under all the various layers of stuff, we are not going to be fully satisfied until all beings are happy.

You may doubt this, thinking you have no genuine wish for the happiness of all beings, yet you may still find, when pushed, that you wish you did have such a desire. If you do, then even that humble wish to want to have a loving heart that desires the happiness of all comes from no other source than the deep heart wish itself. What makes us think we do not wish for the happiness of everyone? It is invariably the idea that it feels pointless. People do not want to articulate it because it seems silly, irrational, and impossible to realize. Nonetheless, underneath everything, it is there and is always there in everyone. From the Buddhist perspective, the explanation is that this is fundamental to what it is to be a sentient being. It is essential to our nature and something that is never not there, never was not there, and never will be not there; in other words, it is never born and never dies. It just is.

If we could simply link into this wish in our hearts in complete simplicity, this would be to rest in the Awakened Heart. But it's hard to be that simple. Doing this to the best of our ability is natural meditation. We don't need any technique more than this really. You could say it is the essence of meditation, free from egocentric concern, resting in the heart's deepest wish without busily trying to do lots of things.

So it is our attitude to our heart wish that is the crucial factor. Are we recognizing it, aligning with it, honouring it, celebrating it? How much is it simply a sentimental idea, and how much is it really being allowed to be active from its own side, shaping all that we are thinking, doing, and saying?

What is interesting is that when we acknowledge this, some kind of inspiration or strength seems to come to us. It is as if we have opened to some power beyond ourselves.

Getting in touch with the heart wish, this place deep inside us that is the source of all our wishes, is at the heart of the path to Awakening and is our surest protection at death. It is the essence of what is called renunciation and what is called devotion, which in Buddhism mean respectively the longing to escape from saṃsāra, and the longing for Awakening. When we stray from the simplicity of that place, this longing becomes distorted into all the ordinary desires that drive the cycle of rebirth in saṃsāra.

But the more we can keep linking back into that deep wordless place from where all wishing comes, the more spontaneously it comes to life within us in an effortless and unconfused way. We find ourselves naturally making good choices, slipping into good attitudes and ways of being, and avoiding bad ones. By relaxing into and trusting the heart wish when we face death, we create a strong momentum that will cause us to keep making the right choices, connecting us to Awakening, in the intermediate state after death and in future lives.

Connecting to the heart

What we mean by 'heart' is multifaceted and rich, and there is much about it that is relevant to how we approach death and thereafter. There seems to be meaning in talking about 'our heart of hearts', 'deep in our heart', 'holding someone in our heart', as if there were some kind of inner sanctum or place of innermost sensitivity. As well as being the seat of our deepest longing, the heart is often associated with warmth and genuineness of feeling, which mean so much at death. When one's whole world and all that it means to you is slipping away, it is only your own and other people's hearts that can offer any sense of meaning at all.

From the Buddhist perspective, however, there is much more to what the heart is than simply the seat of warmth and genuineness – there is a sense in which the heart is the gateway to our innermost being and thus to the true nature of reality. I use the word 'gateway' here because there is a way of connecting to the heart that is akin to entering and letting go into a timeless expanse that is nowhere. It is nowhere, yet somehow it is all-pervading and of immense value. It is more precious than all that pertains to time and space.

This is our essence or true nature, our Awakened Heart, which is not destroyed by death. Since it never changes, since it never came into existence, since it is not conditioned by anything, one can say it is not of the nature of birth and death. It is therefore something we can rely on and trust, in life and in death. There is nothing else we can trust. Everything else will be gone.

This chapter is about how it is our attitude more than anything that matters at the time of death, so we are exploring how it is possible to adopt an attitude that is open to what 'heart' is all about.

Of course, it might not be your particular style to talk much in terms of the heart. Some people are more comfortable with this than others. However, just remembering that way of talking as death approaches can make a tremendous difference. If it doesn't show in the words we choose to use, it may well show in simple things. Sometimes it might show simply in the timing, the way we do things, the pauses, the hesitations, the tone of voice that allow us to connect and meet others in the heart. For the dying that meeting is vital, since all else is about to disappear. Heart connections will be the only connections that are left. For those left behind, that sense of heart connection can be startlingly tangible.

What could connecting to the heart mean in practice? It would include reminding ourselves of the heart and its concerns, trusting the heart to guide us in responding to the whole situation, relaxing into the heart, constantly dipping back into the heart for a few seconds now and then. We may be doing this naturally without thinking of it as a special practice. However we do it, the result is always the same, in that we find a great reservoir of wisdom and courage every time we genuinely connect to the heart. This is available to all of us at any time; it is nearer to us than our own flesh, never more than a heartbeat away. The more you practise connecting to your heart, the more natural it becomes. Such practice is the best preparation for death.

This resting in the heart is total simplicity; an open and trusting heart. The heart at rest in this experience embraces the 'pain' of death and does not blank it out. The pain is felt as excruciating sensitivity that the heart can withstand with equanimity, knowing that it cannot be destroyed by pain. In such a state, pain is no longer pain in the sense of suffering. The pain is its poignant and intense aliveness. If we do not try to shut ourselves off from that pain, we come to recognize its true nature. We train in this in life, and to the extent we can do it in life, we can do it at death. To rest in evenness at death would be to rest in the indestructible compassionate heart of our being. This is to rest in compassion for all beings who share our nature. In that sense the pain of death is not to be shunned, because it is the essence of the heart, beyond pleasure and pain. It is the Awakened Heart itself.

The most important attitude in this context is to open and turn towards the immediate experience of the pain without trying to escape and run away. If we can do this and relax, we become one with the experience and it is no longer pain as such.

To trust one's heart and to open to the pain of death in this way is extremely difficult, and to be able to do it completely takes long training in meditation. Advanced practitioners who trust their heart are delighted to let go of all that is impermanent and unsatisfactory and to open out into the true nature of their being as they die.

For the rest of us, simply to know that this is the ultimate aim of one's practice is an inspiration. To be trying to link into a simple attitude of trusting the heart and not trying to escape from pain can have a beneficial effect at whatever level one practises it. For example, one might be able simply to turns towards the pain with the attitude of not minding it. Even to learn not to mind the fact that you cannot rest in the heart and that you do mind the pain can help, because there is less of a struggle and the situation remains open and simple. Underneath it all there can still be a real sense of peace in the heart and you might even find yourself laughing at yourself and all the fuss you are making.

The message is that our heart can be at ease and happy, even if we fall short of our aims. The fact that we have tried to rest in the heart and tried to let go and turn towards our pain is enough. That was our best shot and it will have had an effect. We can trust that. It is important to have this realistic, down-to-earth attitude at the time of our own death and that of others. This in itself communicates openness, clarity, and sensitivity. Others find it easier to find love, courage, and confidence when we communicate from this underlying trust in the heart.

Sometimes our openness, clarity, and sensitivity tells us to pretend to be braver than we are, or to say that we don't mind things when we do. This is loving and courageous and also helps us to rest in the heart. I think this must be because we are not taking our doubts and fears too seriously. We are letting them go a bit in order to pretend, and that is how we realize we can take them less seriously and let them go.

Trusting the heart and relaxing into the heart is actually more a way of being than an attitude. It expresses itself in different ways at different times. Sometimes it might simply be a matter of being loving and caring towards others. It might take the form of trusting in something intangible yet definite about the nature of one's being, a kind of inner confidence.

For those with faith in the Buddha, Dharma, and Sangha, resting in the heart could simply be a sense of deep commitment to, and love for, the Buddha. Perhaps one calls the true nature of one's being God, so resting in the heart means trusting God. This is quite different from what often goes by the name of faith. Buddhism discourages the panicky clutching at straws of those who try to fend off doubt by clinging to ill-thought-out beliefs. Real faith is a simple, open, relaxed, and humble quality of being. It is a willingness to step open-heartedly into the unknown. This kind of faith comes from the heart and from genuinely following a spiritual path (whether one calls it that or not). This kind of faith helps ourselves and others, in this life, at death, and thereafter.

There is no need to worry about the fact that trust and confidence in the heart are not always focused and clear. Their nature is simply to be there in the background or in the depths of the heart, even when the thinking mind is wandering and unclear. That deep confidence keeps bringing the thinking mind back to a state of calm and stability. We tend to recover ourselves quickly, even if we are thrown off balance. Without this stability, panicky and distraught thoughts and feelings can take us over, increasing our suffering and that of those around us. This is the last thing we need at the time of death.

On the other hand, anybody who has this underlying open-hearted confidence faces death with dignity and courage. From the Buddhist perspective, to be able to die like this is a sign of spiritual accomplishment. It doesn't just happen by accident; it is the result of attitudes cultivated throughout one's life or even lifetimes. So, for anyone who finds this kind of attitude comes easily, it is a sign of a strong connection with the path of Awakening. One does not have to believe this kind of connection is only available to Buddhists, as the heart is the common heritage of all sentient beings. It is the true nature of their being and connects them directly with reality. So connecting to the heart is something that everyone, young or old, saint or criminal, can link into the instant they have the simplicity and humility to do so.

Resolves

Having linked into the heart and accessed our inner resources, there is something more we can do which, from the Buddhist point of view, is of inestimable worth. We can make firm resolves. A resolve is an articulated wish, reinforced by an intention to bring about the desired outcome. It may take the form of a wish, such as 'may we meet again and again,' or a vow, such as 'I will always be with you in my heart.'

In Buddhism, formulating resolves or wishes is a key practice, and it is considered a spiritual accomplishment to be able to make them well. A great deal of attention goes into formulating and reinforcing resolves by means of increasing the confidence, conviction, commitment, and wholeheartedness with which they are made, through repeating them again and again and invoking the power of the truth and the help of Awakened beings and others on the path. This type of special resolve is called *praṇidhāna* in Sanskrit, or *monlam* in Tibetan, often rather weakly translated as 'wishing prayer'.

The Buddhist view is that wishes, intentions, and resolves emanate from the heart wish, and as such are close to the true nature of reality. They have a power in themselves to directly shape the universe and what will happen. The connection between the wish or intention and its outcome does not lie in time or space, so, like any karmic action, its effect can span worlds and lifetimes.

The recognition that we all have this power of resolve is known to all cultures and occurs worldwide in folklore. How many stories can you think of built around the theme of the dying wish? Stories of magic and the casting of spells are examples of the same theme. In Buddhism this power is used to ensure we keep to the path of Awakening and we bring all beings with us, especially those closely connected to us.

Right up to the moment of death, when all else fails us we can still make such a wish. How many stories can you think of where someone has a change of heart at the last minute? Have you noticed how much this means to people? The wish for forgiveness before death finally separates us arises from an intuitive sense that what is in a person's heart continues to have power. From the Buddhist point of view this intuition is accurate, and not just from the psychological point of view.

Karma means action; actions follow from intentions; intentional acts shape the universe. In other words, the basic stuff of the universe is a network of connections not in space and time, but built of our resolves and intentions. What happens to us now rests on what we intended, wished, or resolved in the past, because there is an inescapable connection between our past intentions and deeds and the whole of reality. We ourselves are weaving the magic thread that ensnares us. It is our skilful use of our power of intention and resolve that enables us to break free of that enchantment. Even at our dying breath it is not too late to use that power.

To trust our heart is to trust the power of our intention. The Buddhist tradition teaches many different ways to reinforce the power of our intention and direct it in such a way that it is increasingly in line with our deepest heart wish. This is what connects us to a force that will accompany us at death and ensure future happiness for ourselves and all we love into the indefinite future.

The first step in making a strong praṇidhāna is to acknowledge and align with our heart, which then leads naturally to linking into our power to make resolves based on our heart wish. Anyone can do this, whatever their religious beliefs or lack of them. For example, even if a person does not know whether they believe there is a life to come or not, they might still have an intuitive feeling that it means something to make powerful resolves. The resolves could even be hedged with a provisional 'if'. So one could make the wish that 'if there is some future life, may I always use it to serve others' or 'if there is any way I can atone for the harm I have done, may I never flinch from doing so.' Such a provisional wish is in essence the same as the actual wish and has the same power. All it lacks is the reinforcement that comes of conviction.

Nonetheless, you could instead reinforce it with wholeheartedness. At the very least, making resolves generates a positive attitude of hopefulness and vision, which is the opposite of despair. To despair is to give up hope and adopt a totally negative attitude towards the future. It is the opposite of courage. It is a dispirited attitude. Hopefulness is our life and spirit. It is not the kind of hopefulness with which we try to fool ourselves that the worst is not going to happen. It's the hopefulness of being able to see beyond the worst. It is the hopefulness of linking into the heart wish and having some sense of vision for where that could lead. Hopefulness is another way of saying that we trust our heart and our power of intention and resolve.

It is possible to boost the power of our praṇidhānas by aligning them with the praṇidhānas of Awakened beings, and the Tibetan Buddhist tradition places a lot of emphasis on repeatedly reciting their praṇidhānas. In this way we will make no mistake in what we wish for, and the power of that Awakened being is behind us. Two praṇidhānas I suggest for my students are the Samantabhadracārya prāṇidhāna from the *Avataṃsaka Sūtra*, and the Mahāmudrā prāṇidhāna by Rangjung Dorje.

From the Buddhist perspective, even if we were to do nothing except reflect on what we truly wish for, and make such praṇidhānas from our hearts, we would be helping ourselves and others at the time of death. Making good wishes is something we can encourage others to do. Everyone can do this, even very young children.

Kindness

Even without such resolves, if we have an attitude of being as kind as possible to everyone in whatever way we can, we will not lose our way in life or in death. If we trust our heart, we will naturally be protected and guided by it as well as by those who are Awakened. So we should look on kindness as a lifeline that we will not let go, whatever happens. By adopting the attitude of always treating everyone with kindness, including ourselves, we are automatically linking into the qualities of the heart. Kindness, love, and compassion are the natural expression of the

Awakened Heart, and what we intend and resolve through love and compassion causes us to give up harmful thoughts and cultivate positive ones. Such intentions provoke us to give up selfish attachments and hostility and bring about a happier and more relaxed frame of mind. Such a state of mind is naturally attracted to truth and inspired by the sense of a path to Awakening, even if it is not thinking in those terms exactly. Thus it is a very helpful attitude at the time of death.

Love and compassion are not superficial passing emotions. They are just there. Love is not something that comes and goes. If it comes and goes it's not really love but some kind of transient feeling of like or dislike. Since love is not something that comes and goes, it doesn't die when a person dies. It may seem to come and go, or get stronger or weaker, but it is more that it becomes covered over or blocked. As soon as the obstructions are removed it bursts forth like sunshine.

I think many of us intuit that a person who is full of love does not really die. From the Buddhist perspective, this intuition is accurate, since love is a timeless quality emanating from a person's true nature. Their love is what they most truly are. As their body dies, it's almost as if we can feel their presence and their love more than ever. Of course, we are full of grief at that time, but their love does not die and is somehow able to comfort us because of our openness to it. We meet in the heart.

Meditations for loving kindness

There are many types of meditation practice in the Buddhist tradition that help us link into an attitude of kindness, providing the space for love and compassion to emerge. A particularly good practice for oneself or for others at the time of death is called *tonglen*, which means 'sending and taking'. It means sending out goodness to others and taking suffering on ourselves. It is a practice for increasing our compassion for ourselves and others. I often suggest that people start doing a little of this in preparation for their regular meditation practice and as a method for dealing with any negativity that comes up in their daily lives. The suffering surrounding our own and other people's death gives us plenty of reminders and opportunities to practise tonglen.

It is a practice that can be taught and understood on many levels. For the deeper levels you need proper instruction from a teacher with whom you can discuss it. However, it can be helpful even for someone who has never meditated or who finds it hard to settle to meditation. At the very least it can be a means of overcoming fear and revulsion, the impulse to turn away, run away, or not face up to emotions and unpleasant situations.

In brief, the practice of tonglen consists of opening out to your own suffering so that you experience it fully just as it is, and then breathe it in with the natural rhythm of the in-breath. As you do this, you imagine that the suffering of all other beings is being breathed in with it. This takes courage. The wish to do it springs from love and compassion (even if you do not feel particularly loving and compassionate). Suddenly, as the in-breath fades and gives way to the out-breath, you switch to breathing out all that is good and conducive to happiness, so that it fills your being and flows out to all beings like the light and warmth of the sun.

Many details can be added, such as visualizing the negativity as black, foul, and disgusting, and the good as white, bright, and liquid. The practice can be performed focusing on the specific sufferings and pleasures of individuals in specific situations, or it can be more generalized.

The practice can have all sorts of helpful effects, including undercutting our doubts, fears, and tendency to self-concern and self-pity. As we catch ourselves getting lost in some kind of pathetic storyline, we simply use it as a trigger to breathe in that suffering along with that of everyone else who suffers likewise. There is something tremendously big-hearted and accommodating about practising tonglen. Nothing is too much to be breathed in. It cuts through any tendency to feel overwhelmed or to want to run and hide, ignore, or turn away. At the time of death this is very important, as you need to be able to open right into the situation, however bad it gets. Tonglen is an excellent practice for doing that.

It is also a good way of letting go of attachment, because we breathe out all that we are attached to as happiness for others. There is no time or room for attachment in the practice of tonglen, because you keep switching very suddenly from sending out happiness to taking on suffering. Tonglen completely overturns our selfish and negative tendencies, so that although it is only an exercise and we only do it for a short period at a time, it somehow sets our positive tendencies in motion. Even though the actual practice of tonglen is sometimes quite gruelling, its effects tend to bubble up afterwards as spontaneous feelings of love and compassion and even well-being within us and in those around us.

There are various other Buddhist practices to help us cultivate kindness. One possibility is to recite the *Metta Sutta*, a Buddhist scripture on the subject of spreading loving kindness. There is also a family of quite similar meditation practices for cultivating immeasurable love and compassion that go by names like *mettā-bhāvanā* ('cultivating love'), the *apramāṇas* ('immeasurables') and the *brahma-vihāras* ('divine abodes'). The last verse of the piece called 'Turning the Mind away from Saṃsāra' at the end of this book contains a brief reminder of the *apramāṇas* meditation. Just to read the lines and reflect on them is good, but for full instruction you really need a teacher.

I wrote the following lines a few years ago to be read as a simple tonglen practice at the time of death:

> *Contemplating death,*
> *Do not fear it,*
> *But learn to trust*
> *What is not touched by it.*

Contemplating others,
Rest in the heart's wish to truly know them,
A longing to know what they truly need,
And what will bring them happiness.

Breathe deeply into that place
Where all hearts meet.
Remain bound in love
Until all sorrows cease.

Breathe out a continuous flow
Of warmth from the heart,
Providing each and every being
With exactly what they need,
Now and forever.

No being and no form of suffering
Is excluded from this prayer.
No suffering is too great to be encompassed by it,
No being too wretched or unworthy.

Open your heart and take on all suffering and all beings.
Let go of doubts and hesitations.
Let the power of the Awakened Heart flow through you,
Now and forever.

May all distress subside,
May all that is lacking be provided,
May all that is wayward be tamed,
May all that needs destroying be destroyed.

Giving

Wishes, intentions, and resolves, together with an attitude of
kindness, will naturally spill over into generous actions which
are, from the Buddhist point of view, extremely efficacious for
our own good as well as for others, especially at the time of
death.

Perhaps we are not used to thinking of giving as something that is going to benefit ourselves more than those we give to. Generally speaking, we in the West think that our reason for giving should simply be to benefit others. From the Buddhist point of view, such an attitude to giving makes the gift even more efficacious in terms of its benefit to ourselves, since it is not in any way tainted with self-interest. I think this intuitively feels right to us. There are many fairy tales of people who have benefited by their unselfish acts of giving. This intuition is right, because giving (whether for our own sake or for the sake of others) is the best way to provide for our welfare in future lives. So at death, Buddhists will be very eager to make gifts of all kinds. Some of the giving will be on the part of the person dying, and some of it on behalf of the deceased by those who are left behind.

In line with the general thrust of this chapter, one can look on giving as simply the expression of openness, clarity, and sensitivity. When we open to others, our impulse is naturally to give, whether it be a smile, a cup of tea, or a more substantial gift of our time and resources. The goodness that comes from the giving of gifts and other good deeds is called *puṇya* (often weakly translated as merit). This goodness is thought of as something with power in its own right that can itself be given away or dedicated. In Buddhist countries, many of the customs surrounding death are about gathering and giving away puṇya in order to reinforce the power of the praṇidhānas being made at that time. Even though we might not be thinking this as we make our gifts, from the Buddhist perspective, the goodness is still there and having its influence in the fulfilment of our wishes.

Rather than thinking in terms of puṇya, I think we westerners tend to be more focused on the psychological effect of the gift on both the giver and the recipient and the immediate benefits of the gift. So, for example, the giving and receiving of gifts is a way of honouring another person and expressing our love, a way of giving up grasping and selfishness, a way of feeling empowered to do something tangible to help in a difficult situation.

We have plenty of customs that express generosity, such as giving care and hospitality, cards and messages of sympathy and condolence, making gifts to charities, lighting a candle accompanied by a prayer, giving flowers to add cheer or as a sign of respect, or, even more tellingly, to leave at the place where a person has died or on their grave. It is hard to decide exactly why we do these last things, unless it's from an intuitive sense that giving is good in itself, even if there is nobody to receive the gift. Maybe we do these things as a kind of statement to those left behind, expressing our feelings of love and respect, perhaps in the same way as we make gifts and create foundations in a person's memory.

As a Buddhist, one could think of all these acts of generosity as producing puṇya, which can be dedicated in order to reinforce the effectiveness of our praṇidhānas. In one's mind, one could gather up all the puṇya of the giving that occurs in connection with a person's death (whether one's own or that of another) and dedicate it to the Awakening of all beings.

The message here is that, whether one has Buddhist beliefs or not, there is something intuitively right about making gifts and practising generosity around a person who is dying or has died. From the Buddhist point of view, the more we go with this intuition, the greater the benefit for ourselves and others, both in this life and in future lives. It is a Buddhist belief that such gifts actually help the person who has died while they wander in the intermediate state after death and help them find a good rebirth in which they can continue to follow the path to Awakening.

Buddhists actually welcome the time of death as an opportunity to give all they have and dedicate the goodness of that to the Awakening of all beings. We might long to give up all we possess in order to give up attachment and to benefit others, but this is usually impractical, as we still need the means to care for ourselves and our dependants. However, at death there is nothing to stop us giving up everything with a joyful and non-attached heart.

Receiving

The other side of giving is receiving. Sometimes it is more generous to receive than to give, as it allows others to give and this benefits them. So as well as taking every opportunity to give and dedicate the goodness of giving for the benefit of the person who is dying, one should take every opportunity to allow and help others to give too.

This is helpful advice to anyone who has a fatal illness and is being cared for by others. If at that time we can trust our heart and give up our pride that tells us that we shouldn't have to depend on others, we can open to them and let them feel our gratitude. This reinforces the very tendencies in them that will bring them benefit and happiness. So we can dedicate the goodness arising from that in the same way that we would dedicate our own acts of generosity. So, lying there physically helpless, one can still be creating heart connections that will be of immense benefit to them in this and future lives, simply by one's attitude and intentions.

We could go further than this by deliberately and systematically thinking of all the kindness of parents, teachers, family members, and mentors who brought us up and showed us how to live a good life. This would include all those who have taught us the way to follow the path to Awakening. Thinking of their generosity and kindness, and the kindness of all who have helped us during our lifetime, fosters an attitude of gratitude and a great wish to repay that kindness with countless acts of generosity and kindness. If we find ourselves dying with such an attitude, we have very little to worry about. Such an attitude is in itself a sign that we are resting in our heart and are naturally under the protection of the Awakened Ones.

Once it ceases to grasp and cling, generosity and gratitude are the natural states of our being. Grasping and clinging always bring suffering, especially at death, when all is taken from us. By letting go of grasping, having a generous and grateful attitude, we allow our heart to breathe freely and its deeper wisdom and confidence to emerge, so the importance of generosity and gratitude can never be stressed enough.

Heart connections with others

An attitude of respecting and valuing our heart connections with others is an important part of what it means to trust the heart. From a Buddhist perspective, our connections with others go very deep; they are part of the very fabric of the essence of our being and of the universe.

I use the phrase 'heart connection' partly to refer to the intuitive sense that we naturally feel towards certain people, and partly to refer to the inescapable heart connection we have with all beings. In other words, to have a heart connection to all other beings is fundamental to the nature of what it is to be a being. When we intuitively feel that connection with some people more than others, it is simply that we are more aware of it with some people. You could say that in some mysterious sense all beings are connected in the heart, so our heart connections are with all beings.

Sometimes people misinterpret Buddhist teachings on non-attachment to mean that we should try to give up our heart connections to friends and family. It can be misinterpreted to mean that all love of this kind is a form of desire and attachment that needs to be abandoned. However, it is taught that our connections to those we love pass from lifetime to lifetime, so it is important to honour and respect those connections and reinforce them with powerful praṇidhānas and resolves so that we can meet again and again in auspicious circumstances. In particular, if we are followers of the path to Awakening, we make praṇidhānas to meet and help each other again and again in all future lives.

Until we are Awakened, it is only natural that our love will be mixed with desire and attachment, and it is the desire and attachment, not the heart connection, that will cause suffering at the time of death. At the time of death, we see only too clearly the difference between our attachment to outward illusory forms and the joy of recognizing our genuine heart connections. It is our heart connections that bring us comfort and inspiration. I think it is fairly common for people, after the initial shock of bereavement, to draw great strength from the timelessness of this deeper connectedness.

People who are about to die often have an intuitive sense of the importance of those connections, and they want to make peace with others. This attitude of keeping good faith and repairing damaged connections reinforces our sense of their importance and helps us die with confidence, with a heart at peace. From the Buddhist perspective our connections with others are inescapable. Even connections that have brought us suffering continue after death, so it is important to make a strong resolve (*praṇidhāna*) to improve those difficult relationships in future lives.

Those who are very close to us are our best means for discovering the nature of our connectedness with other beings. On the basis of these heart connections, we can gradually come to recognize that ultimately we have that same connection with all beings. This is the importance and ultimate significance of the deep heart connections we feel we have with certain people. When death divides us, we have to let go, but that doesn't mean that deep connection is meaningless. On the contrary, it means we should use that heart connection to deepen our connections with all beings.

At death, a strong sense of opening to and relying on our heart connections offers us some kind of protection. It gives us a sense of groundedness in a reality other than the one the death process is stripping away. It is worth mentioning here that, since these connections are more fundamental to our being than those aspects of it that are conditioned by this life, they have a power from their own side. This means that when we open our hearts and trust those connections, we are grounded in a reality that has the power to support us even after death. Maybe these undying qualities of our heart connections are what people intuit when they open themselves to another person and say, 'I will love you forever.'

The Buddhist perspective I am describing here is not something we can really know for ourselves at the outset. There is nothing in Buddhism that says you have to take this kind of thing on as a kind of belief system, but perhaps one could take it on as a kind of inspiration. These are things that we will be able to understand properly only when we become fully Awakened. But we can perhaps sense some meaning here, feeling that all this is true to what we most value and trust in life.

Don't panic

Having said all this about the importance of our attitude when we die, and how we need to trust our heart and rely on our heart connections and let go, when it comes to the actual moment, perhaps all we will be able to remember is this one simple phrase, 'Don't panic!' This is the vital point. If you forget all else, don't forget this.

The more we can die with an underlying attitude of relaxed confidence, the less likely we are to panic and lose our way. We will be able to continue on the path to Awakening from life to life for as long as it takes, always meeting Dharma companions and teachers and being helped along the path to Awakening.

How can we be sure? I suppose there is always room for doubt. But, when the chips are down, we have to trust or panic, don't we? Well, let's not panic. Let's trust. But trust what? We can learn to trust our heart, our true nature, our own inner wisdom, love and compassion, heart connections. That is possible. But is that enough to keep us on the path to Awakening? From the Buddhist perspective, it is. If we fully trust that and don't panic, it is enough. It is enough because it is our true nature and therefore trustworthy. It is enough because even without knowing it, if we align ourselves with our hearts, we are naturally open to the power (*adhiṣṭhāna*) of the living reality of Awakening. This manifests as the protection of all the Awakened Ones, who are there for us even if we do not recognize them or believe in them. We can believe in them or not, just as we like. They will still help us.

So we should never feel discouraged, for the sake of ourselves and for others, if we find ourselves at death's door unprepared. Just remember the mottos 'don't panic,' 'relax,' 'take each step as it comes,' 'too late to worry,' 'don't try to hang on to anything, let go, now is the time to let it all go,' 'trust the goodness of your own heart,' 'trust your heart connection to those you love,' 'look for the path to Awakening.' There are as many ways of putting it as there are people. The important thing is to find a way of putting it that gives you confidence and allows you to relax and not panic, whatever happens.

The interesting thing is that when we are scared and then decide to stop panicking, we feel disorientated for a moment and then suddenly some kind of basic sanity or basic groundedness kicks in. It is just there underneath all the panic and hysteria, biding its time. Sooner or later our panic comes to an end and there is that sanity. This underlying reality of basic sanity, the truth of the heart, is present in all of us, and this is what we can trust at death.

FIVE

Relating to your mind at death

I have talked about the attitudes it is good to develop when moving towards death, but what, in practice, should we do at the actual time of death? What does opening to our experience and having confidence in it mean at that time? How do we make sure that we link into the heart, and what practical steps can we take to prevent ourselves panicking?

The answer is that it is simply a matter of taking each moment as it comes without obsessively thinking we shouldn't be experiencing this, or things should not be like this or that. In other words, we take things in our stride. Whatever the present experience, it's a matter of recognizing that that's how it is and that's fine. That's what I will practise with. So if it is pain, fear, attachment, anger, depression, jealousy, uncontrollable thoughts, worries, regrets, weariness, dullness, loneliness, sadness, drowsiness, or confusion, that is the experience I am opening to from my heart. All I have to do is let go of the complications of thinking and be as relaxed as possible, trusting my connection to the path of Awakening. When the experiences are good, such as feelings of love, tenderness, joy, peace, calm, compassion, and faith in the Dharma, Dharma teachers, and companions, then again it's a matter of simply experiencing them as they are. I just have to trust my heart and relax without getting attached to hopes and fears about trying to make such states last. When they change, I simply open to the next experience and trust its essence to be same true nature of awareness. The

essence of awareness itself is always the same, whether one recognizes it as such or not. In the end, having a strong underlying
confidence in this is all that matters.

Thoughts and emotions

In practice, this means catching yourself before you get caught
up in too much thinking (for example, worrying about what is
going to happen well past the point where anything can be
gained by it), or, on the other hand, trying to clamp down on it.

Thinking is driven by emotion, and emotions are connected with
the body. The body is going through physical changes which
produce strong emotional responses, and these responses
include strong fear reactions, which again express themselves in
physical reactions. These days, we have medication to relieve
some of these symptoms. Nevertheless, irreversible changes are
under way and we are heading for the unknown. This in itself
produces emotional changes, such as a heightened sense of
awareness and even delight in the wonder of life. The emotions
can make us hypersensitive, so that we become angry with our
loved ones because of perceived slights and insensitivities, or we
might feel guilty about the trouble we are putting them through
because of our mood swings and neediness. Whatever the emotions, they naturally whip up lots of thinking, and a part of us
wants somehow to clamp down on the thinking and emotion in
order to have some sense of peace. But the more we try to do that,
the more the thinking bursts out or makes us feel tense and out of
touch with our experience.

So we need to recognize that trying to control the situation
beyond what is possible is simply clinging to an idea, and if we
do not let that idea go we will end up causing unnecessary suffering to ourselves and those around us. Graciously letting go of
control as the body deteriorates, and relying more and more on
others, is a wonderful opportunity for Dharma practice. The path
of Awakening is all about giving up pride and attachment to our
idea of what we are and letting all that go. The intense suffering

of the dying process can help us recognize how deeply we cling to our idea of self and our need for control. It is possible to look on death as our teacher, showing us what we need to recognize and let go. So instead of being angry with ourselves for thinking too much, for getting angry, for feeling needy, for being tense, for being hypersensitive, or whatever else we are experiencing, we can give up trying to control and justify ourselves, give up trying to blame ourselves or others, and instead just stay with the experience exactly as it is in a kind, gentle, and even grateful way. This is actually the essence of meditation.

Some meditation exercises

For those who wish to follow the path of Awakening but have never had any meditation instruction, I suggest the following exercise. I recommend this even to quite experienced meditators who find it hard to meditate at the time of death.

Open to your experience by repeatedly bringing your attention back to the rhythm of the breath, especially the out-breath, or to the actual physical sensations of the body. This helps bring the attention into the present moment, forcing you to let go of distracted thinking. It can be amazingly difficult to keep your attention fixed on a sensation for even a few seconds when you feel upset or disturbed by something. So it is important to be content with even a modest amount of success. Sometimes, simply to keep trying to come back into the present, even with little more than momentary success, can help us let go of obsessive thinking, slow us down, and allow a gap, so that some more appropriate response to the situation can bubble up.

If you feel very disturbed, you could pay attention to the breath or the sensations in the body for just a minute or two at a time, and see how that goes. If you repeat this exercise as frequently as possible, you might start to notice you have a kind of power to do something about your mind. You might not be able to focus for long, but if you get interested in the breath or a physical sensation, or even in the fact that it is really difficult to keep your attention fixed in this way, you will start to discover something about your mind. You might discover that you have more choice about how to relate to your experience than you thought, which is subtly different from trying to hold on to things and control situations that cannot be controlled. In other words, you might notice the possibility of some kind of inner peace and freedom, even in the midst of pain and suffering.

Although the practice of meditation is a big topic that cannot be covered in a few lines, even if you have never tried meditation before, just a few minutes of quietly trying to get your attention to home in on the breath or some other physical sensation can connect you to your basic sanity for a moment, and this can have quite a strong effect. It might even have the effect of entirely shifting your mood, but even if it doesn't, you are still making a move that connects you more strongly to the path of Awakening.

One of the effects of even a few moments of meditative aware-ness is that one is less driven by all the thoughts carrying on inside one's head. I say 'inside one's head' because we tend to think that is where they are – as if we lived in a little cave behind our eyes that is full of unruly thoughts and feelings. It is possible to notice that one has this idea, and to notice it is actually just an idea. It is as if we think of ourselves as a little person living inside our heads, but that cannot literally be true, can it?

Our thoughts extend out into space, our awareness can contain thoughts that stretch to the horizon and beyond. That is too much space to be inside our heads. If you can let go of the idea that you are in your head, even for a moment, you could try to let your awareness expand into a vaster and vaster sense of space in which your experience is happening. When we do this, we might experience a kind of resistance – a kind of mental and physical tensing. It is good to notice that and somehow let it go a bit. The remarkable thing is that simply to think about doing this in a relaxed way produces some effect. We intuitively sense that we can open out into space and relax, and, if we can do it even for a fraction of a second, it feels good. To play with this sense of spaciousness intrinsic to the nature of our being enables us to open to and trust the path of Awakening.

Another meditative exercise is to bring your awareness into your heart. One way to do this is just to notice that when you think 'heart', there is a movement of awareness as it drops into your heart. Having done this, try opening out from there into a sense of space.

Once your awareness is opening out from the heart into space, when thoughts arise, they do so in that open-hearted space of awareness as subtle movements. It is possible just to let them be in that space without trying to stop them or getting lost in them. The same goes for the feelings and sensations.

Feelings and sensations

Even when you are in a lot of pain, you can let the pain be there while you relax into your heart and the space of awareness. When we are in pain, we think about how awful it is and how we want it to stop, and how to stop it getting worse, and what to do if it does, and so on. This is where it really helps to see that those are thoughts, and that you can relax and let the thoughts come and go. Even 'I hate this' or 'I can't stand this' are thoughts you could let be.

When intense feelings arise, let any associated thoughts come and go and simply home in on the feeling. As you do this you might find yourself wondering what exactly the feeling is, or where exactly it is, which brings the attention right into the moment. You might notice that this changes the experience quite significantly.

This is how to turn towards your experience: let it be, let it go, or let it come and go. In this way you come to recognize that there is more to your experience than the racing thoughts and the feelings that drive them. You are more than all this, bigger than all this. You are your awareness, and awareness is boundless and a wellspring of some kind of wisdom that can just bubble up with fresh responses moment by moment. This is something we can all discover in ourselves and learn to have confidence in, so that even in the eleventh hour we can find some kind of trust in our connection to the path of Awakening.

Meditative exercises such as these help us to cultivate the states of mind we need at the time of death, such as openness, open-heartedness, equanimity, fearlessness, confidence, and so on.

In effect, what we are doing is opening up sufficiently for there to be a gap in the thinking process through the simple act of being willing to stay with our breath or sensations for a moment or two, a minute or two, five or ten minutes or so, at regular intervals.

It might sound as if I think that this is easy. Maybe it is for you. However, it is usually very hard. It is not hard because it's difficult in itself; it is hard because we lack conviction, so we easily give up on it. We easily allow negative thoughts to convince us that there is no use in trying to practise in this way. We are very influenced by our thoughts. That is why in Buddhism we are encouraged to train throughout our lives to notice our thoughts and to not let them drive us, so that this simple practice becomes easier and easier. When we are no longer driven by our thoughts, we can let go of doubts and hesitations and trust our connection to the path of Awakening when we die. We have the freedom to choose what we want to think, and therefore to choose whatever practice we think best for us to do as we die.

Valuing our glimpses

Our true nature is just that: what we really are. Therefore we are never far from it, and most of us have moments in which we have some sense of it, however faint. For example, we are all familiar with the dream metaphor applied to life's experiences when what is happening to us doesn't seem quite 'real'. We say things like, 'it all passed like a dream,' or 'I felt I was living in a dream.' I think what we mean when we say this kind of thing is that we feel an odd sense of unreality that we cannot quite put our finger on. There was probably a flash of insight to trigger that kind of remark, but not strong enough to have much effect unless we recognize and value it. At other times, when looking back at the past, remembering those who have passed away, or remembering times and places long gone, we can sometimes experience a strange and intense poignant moment in which it all seems to have been like a dream. This would be a stronger momentary flash of insight.

Valuing such insights and cultivating them, by reflecting on them and letting their significance sink in and permeate our being, enables them to arise more frequently and with greater effect. The way to cultivate them is to make resolves or aspirations to recognize them and their significance more and more clearly. As Natsok Rangdröl says (*The Mirror of Mindfulness*, p.83),

> *Aspiration, in particular, is of the utmost importance as the essential point of all the dream and bardo trainings. This means that one should be continuously mindful and determined, thinking: 'What I do now is like a dream and illusion!... All my experiences are bardo experiences! I should apply the specific key points of practice!' With such determination one cannot avoid being adept in the bardo.*
>
> *Most ordinary people, however, are solidly fixated, thinking: 'These present experiences are completely real! They are actual! I am not dead!'*

We shouldn't be discouraged, thinking our moments of insight are too short and fleeting to be of use or that we are unable to sustain or rest in that state of awareness. Those glimpses are not in time, so it is only our thinking that makes them seem short. And it is only our thinking that makes the time between them seem long.

By way of encouragement, it's worth noting that Urgyen Tulku repeatedly says in his book, *As It Is*, that at death, a practitioner needs only to maintain awareness of the Clear Light (our true nature) for a few seconds, and that is enough to attain liberation. Although our glimpses may not compare with those of an advanced practitioner who can gain liberation as they dissolve in the Clear Light at death, they are still powerful and have a profound effect on our world-view and our connection with the path to Awakening.

Choosing your Death Dharma

Even though we always need to keep death in mind as we practise the Dharma, while we are alive we have many things to think of and perhaps different ways of practising in different circumstances. So from time to time it is good to reflect on which of these you feel most confident in when it comes to facing the moment of death. Although it's wise to plan as if we were to live for years ahead, we do this in the knowledge that death might come at any time. So it is important to think right now about what we have most faith in and make sure we are ready to practise that when faced with imminent death.

In the Tibetan tradition this is called one's Death Dharma. Think, for example, what comes to mind when you see a car coming straight towards you and you think you are about to die. Try to be ready for that moment, so that when you see the danger your first thought is something that connects you to the path of Awakening. You might, for example, cry 'Buddha!' or think of a mantra. You could train yourself to utter a short prayer such as 'Buddha I put my trust in you,' or 'I take Refuge in the Buddha, Dharma, and Sangha.' It might simply be 'may I never forget the Awakened Heart,' 'may I always be able to help all beings,' or 'may I realize that this is all like a dream.' Whatever it is, make sure you have a short version of it that you can link into very strongly when you are sick or in danger.

SIX

Trusting our connection to the path

Whereas up to this point I have been writing mainly about what kind of attitudes and behaviour are helpful at death, this and the following chapter are intended for those who have decided to follow the path and want more specific guidance on how to practise at death. In a nutshell, my advice when your time comes is to do the practice in which you have most confidence. From now on, make sure you practise every day as though preparing to do it at the moment of death. Then, when the moment of death comes, link into that practice with confidence by doing it in the usual way.

These days we can choose from a range of Buddhist practices from a range of Buddhist traditions, as literature on them is so freely available. This bewildering array of choice is unprecedented and presents problems that would not have arisen in the past. Traditional Buddhists would probably have been following one particular branch of one tradition, and just one teacher. Even then, the range of teachings and practices on offer might have seemed too much, and they might have requested just one instruction from that teacher to see them through both life and death.

So what should we do if we don't have that one tradition, teacher, or instruction? I suggest we have no recourse but to make our own choice and stick to it with conviction. I say this because otherwise we can end up doing one thing but thinking we should be doing something else (a problem for many of us anyway). So we need to train to trust our convictions and connections. This doesn't mean trusting a set of beliefs or ideas. It means trusting our honesty, inner strength, and sense of meaning.

Furthermore, the reader may already be aware of various elaborate practices that are recommended, especially for the time of death, particularly in the Tibetan Buddhist tradition, and be wondering whether to use them. The message I always try to put across is that the efficacy of these elaborate practices depends on complete faith and conviction in what one is doing. There is unlikely to be much use in suddenly engaging in a special, but unfamiliar, practice at the time of death. If you have a practice that you can do with confidence and conviction, it is better to stick with that. What we need to do in this life is to practise the path in order to gain conviction in it, and then rely on that conviction and connection to the path at the time of death. We can trust in that connection alone, and do not really need further elaborate practices specially for death. This is what my own teachers have advised me, and it is what Natsok Rangdröl emphasizes again and again. In his parting words of advice he writes, 'concentrate on practising whatever you incline towards or are familiar with.'

I stress that trusting in our connection with the path is enough, because death is often preceded by a period of pain, suffering, and uncertainty, when it is sometimes very hard to meditate or keep calm and clear. Think about what happens when you are ill, even if it is only a cold, and notice how hard it is to remain clear-headed and meditate. As I often say about myself, 'As a practitioner, I have my good days and my bad days. I expect the day I die will be one of my bad days.' I don't mind that, because I trust my connection to the path and believe that, whatever happens, I will be able to resume the practice at some point.

Yet there are ways of making even a difficult situation into the path of Awakening. Notice what helps you keep to the path in that kind of situation, and make up your mind to practise at death in the same way. Most of us just give up when we have a cold and put our heads under the covers intending to practise again once we feel better. We end up relying on our commitment to start again as soon as our head is clear. So at that time, in effect, our practice is to trust ourselves and our connection to the path. That is exactly what we need to be thinking and feeling as we die.

Feeling confident in ourselves and the path in this way is what it means to trust our connection to the path. It is enough. Do not undermine that confidence by getting anxious, thinking that you are not doing enough. Instead of getting anxious, keep affirming your intention to meditate again as soon as you can, and engage yourself in positive thoughts that keep you connected to the path. It is important to be realistic and not to have unrealistic expectations as we approach death. Instead, we need to put energy into our practice now so that we have a strong connection to the path that will go with us as we enter the gateway of death. This is because the path of Awakening has a power from its own side to help us, so our connection to it is something we can rely on whatever happens to our mind.

A remedy for egocentric thinking

I once thought being a Buddhist meant completely dispensing with any sense of a higher power that could help me from its own side. For a long time I thought the power of the Dharma all lay in my own thinking. If this were true, the question arises as to how Awakening could be anything other than a mental creation. As such, the path to Awakening would consist of thoughts alone, so in the intermediate state after death we would have only the power of our own thinking to rely on. It is very hard to see how this would liberate us from egocentric thinking and fear of losing control at the time of death.

I once met someone who had a lot of experience of people as they died, and he said it was often priests and Buddhists who suffered most, because they felt they were spiritual failures, not really able to trust in anything and let go of this life peacefully. I suppose what had happened is that they had been relying solely on their ability to control their own minds, without trusting that reality had a power to help from its own side. What they needed to do was trust in their connection to the true nature of reality, and relax. This contrasts with other people around someone approaching death reporting that they change; they gave up their egocentric preoccupations and seemed to link into and trust something other than their usual self, in a way they had never previously been able to.

You might wonder why, if there is so much power in just having a connection to the path, one would bother to strive for Awakening with so much effort. Where do great practitioners get the motivation to put sufficient energy into their practice? There are two main sources of inspiration. One is the clarity of realizing there is nothing else worth striving for, and that the pain of not Awakening is too excruciating to bear any longer than necessary. The other is this clarity combined with deep compassion for others. In other words, one realizes that one cannot continue to be helpless when faced with the sufferings of others.

In order to realize one's full potential to help others, one must fully Awaken as soon as possible. So the genuine motivation for striving to realize Awakening in this life or at death is deep wisdom and compassion. If we have such wisdom and compassion, then we need to trust that and not get anxious, filling our minds with doubt and worry, at the time of death. Instead, we need to relax and trust our connection to the path of Awakening.

When teaching Buddhism it's always difficult to balance this message of putting one's trust in the power of one's connection to the path, with the need to get people out of their complacency and to put energy into the path to Awakening. Tibetan teachers, for example, spend much time stressing the horrors of saṃsāra and the dangers that lurk beyond death, trying to get people worried so that they put energy into their practice. This kind of emphasis is important for people like their students, who might have so much faith in the power of the Dharma and their connection with it that they become lazy about putting it into practice.

As a Dharma teacher in the West, I find myself in a completely different situation. My students are not sure whether they believe in future lives, or that they will be able to continue to follow the path to Awakening after death. But they still have to face death, and all the questions it throws up. They can find inner confidence through practising meditation and their conviction grows year by year, but death can strike at any time. What are they going to do now, at their present stage? That is what I will address in this chapter.

There is a tendency for westerners to be attracted to Buddhism because of its emphasis on direct experience and meditation. It offers a means of discovering truth for oneself rather than expecting us to adopt a whole system of beliefs. This can make us think that only in meditation, when we have a calm and clear mind, are we practising Dharma. As this kind of thinking can cause panic when our mind is disturbed at death, it is important to think of Dharma practice in broader terms. As well as meditation, it could of course mean a whole range of practices for fostering the attitudes and behaviour mentioned in the previous chapter, as well as a further range of elaborate practices found within the Buddhist tradition. But it could also mean simply having an underlying trust in our connection to the path. As we die, we could still be making progress towards Awakening, even if we are not able to do anything in particular, because we are connected to the path of Awakening and it has power from its own side.

The power of our connection to the path

If we trusted our connection with the path to Awakening, in what would we be trusting? On the one hand, we could simply be talking about trust in ourselves and our true nature. On the other hand, we could be talking about trust in the power of the path and our connection to it in the sense of both having power from its own side. You could perhaps think of it like a magnet. This power is called *adhiṣṭhāna* in Sanskrit, which is often weakly translated as 'blessing'.

As westerners we tend to think of trust in our connection to the path as a kind of psychological trick, as if all the power came from our own thinking. Ultimately this is not very reassuring. From the Buddhist perspective we are right to see that there must to be more to it than that. However, if we intuitively recognize that there is a reality beyond all our concepts – even such fundamental concepts as time, space, self, other, existence and non-existence – then that reality must have a power from its own side. So what is the power of our connection with it?

When talking about heart connections, I pointed out that these connections are not in space or time, and yet are more meaningful and important than anything we know. I also indicated that the connection between a karmic act and its outcome is outside space and time, otherwise there could be no connection from one life to the next. Similarly, the connection with the path of Awakening that we can trust at death is outside space and time. It is timeless and indestructible. One could argue that, as with karma and heart connections, analysed intellectually, these connections cannot pass from life to life. Nevertheless, we might intuitively sense that it means something in those terms. In fact, it is possible to trust that intuition. It is not very different from trusting our intuition that people are not just figments of our imagination. I am not sure I could prove it intellectually, but I trust it implicitly in the way I relate to my experience. I would be considered mad if I didn't!

Once one has taken on board that our fundamental nature is ungraspable openness, clarity, and sensitivity, it is not such a big leap to think that we can make a connection with that nature and it could have a power from its own side to draw us to Awakening. Even though we might be unable to realize the true nature of our being before we die, we can at least trust our connection with the path to its realization.

I am using the word 'path' here in a special way. When we talk of the truth that the Buddha taught (the Dharma) as a path, we mean the teachings that point to that truth, the practices that open us to that truth, and the power the Dharma awakens within us to draw us to that truth. In other words, there is a power in the Dharma itself that draws us to it, and this is something we can trust.

According to this way of thinking, every movement that connects us to the truth (the Dharma) opens us to its influence in a very deep way. From our point of view, it might seem to be just a psychological matter of managing our mind but, from the point of view of reality (the Dharma), something has happened that is timelessly imprinted in the structure of the universe. That movement in our mind, in harmony with the living truth itself, allows that truth or reality to draw us towards it. This might not be immediately detectable, but from the point of view of ultimate reality (Dharma), when we connect to it through our thoughts or actions, something always happens within the true nature of reality at a deeper level than we are aware of. In other words, we are changed by that connection and so is our future.

This makes sense when one thinks of how the root of saṃsāra is our loss of connection with the true nature of reality. Obviously our turning towards reality and reconnecting to it by, for example, opening out towards our experience, is going to cut at the very root of saṃsāra. What we are actually doing is aligning with the truth and drawing on its power. This is the power that reality has from its own side that has nothing to do with the egocentric efforts of our thinking mind. Practising Dharma turns out to be a matter of aligning with and cooperating with reality itself, as if we are creating cracks in the armour of our delusion through which the energy of the Awakened Heart can pour through. A tiny chink might not seem like much, but it doesn't take many cracks to burst a dam.

This is all bold talk. I am speaking here from the point of view of the Mahāmudrā, Dzogchen, and other practice traditions. Nonetheless, one can find teachings in line with this way of thinking in many parts of the Buddhist tradition, especially in rituals and customs, and in the stories of great practitioners.

At the time of death it is easy to panic and feel we are in free fall, alone and exposed to a hostile universe. This sense of things breaking up and disappearing might happen again and again during the intermediate state, so it is very important to have confidence that we are connected to the path of Awakening right through this experience. If we can remain confident and don't panic, we will find ourselves coming out on the other side of the experience still able to follow that path. Whatever appears to us, whatever experience arises, we just need the confidence to regard it as a passing display generated by the mind, and that if we do not shy away and try to escape from it, we are more likely to be able to recognize it as such. Our only alternative is to try to separate ourselves from the experience and run. But since it is our own mind, we cannot escape it. Running and hiding is likely to make our mind seem more threatening than ever. All our ordinary connections that related to this world break up as we die, so we have only our timeless connection to reality and the path to rely on.

You might be wondering whether this means that unless you are a Buddhist you cannot connect to the path of Awakening. The answer is that the path of Awakening is a power inherent in the nature of the universe, and anyone who finds that path is on it, whether they call themselves Buddhist or not. It is unnecessary to think that only those who call themselves Buddhists can find the genuine path of Awakening. Those who are following the Dharma in principle are connected to the path of Awakening, whether they call themselves Buddhists or not. There is nothing in Buddhism to say that the Dharma cannot find its way to us through a tradition that did not go by the name of Buddhism, or even that it cannot find its way to us without our belonging to any spiritual tradition at all.

This is because Awakening or Dharma is actually reality, which is everywhere, all the time. It is a living reality, the living truth, not just a set of words passed on by Buddhists. It is intrinsic to the nature of the universe. But the chance of discovering it without the help of others is remote. That is why making a strong living connection with those who are deeply connected to the path is so important.

Once we have such a connection with the path of Awakening, it is there whether or not we believe it, whether or not we feel relaxed at death. Of course, it would be great to feel relaxed and be able to simply rest in our direct experience at that time, but even if we didn't, the connection with the path to Awakening would still be there. Accepting this as fact might help us relax; we do not even have to worry about whether or not we can trust it, whether or not we have faith in it, whether or not we deserve help. The power of Awakening is interested in us, whoever we are and whether or not we are interested in it.

Worries about karma

Traditionally, Buddhist teachers stress that in order to ensure a safe passage through death to happy rebirths, it is crucial to have done as many good karmic acts as possible and to have repented all the negative ones. While I would not argue with this, you might find it reassuring to know that if one can trust one's connection to the path of Awakening, then one must already have a great deal of good karma and one must have repented having transgressed against it.

In fact, our choices regarding our situation at the time of death are exactly the same regardless of how much good or bad karma we made in the past. We are all in an equally uncertain situation, since we have all performed limitless numbers of good and bad actions in the course of our countless lives, and we don't know when their effects will ripen. Whether our next karmic consequences will be good or bad, all we can actually do in practice is to trust our connection with the path of Awakening.

You might wonder whether your connection to the path of Awakening is strong enough, whether you have done enough, but you don't need to worry in this way. Not having done enough cannot invalidate what you have done and are doing. It is true that the more we have done (or others have dedicated for us) to strengthen our connection, the easier our journey will be. But as long as we trust our connection with the Dharma, we can rest assured that we are on the right path and, although we might have a bumpy ride, we are well on our way in the right direction. Trusting the heart and trusting our connection to the path of Awakening are the main things. The rest is extra. From the Buddhist perspective, the very fact that you have that kind of trust means you must have done enough to point in the right direction.

Buddhist scriptures often emphasize the rarity of obtaining a human birth instead of a less fortunate birth without opportunities to practise Dharma. In order to motivate people to practise Dharma they place great stress on it being very difficult to obtain otherwise. For example, one famous text, the *Bodhicaryāvatāra* (1.iv), says

> *Now that I have this rare freedom and opportunity to practise*
> *Dharma,*
> *I have the chance to accomplish the true purpose of human life.*
> *If I waste it, what chance is there that I will have it again in the*
> *future?*

Because of these teachings, I have come across sincere and earnest Buddhist practitioners who feel their only chance is to reach Awakening in this very life, or at least at death. Unfortunately they overlook the fact that these teachings also say that once we have put our trust in the path of Awakening, we are assured of future opportunities to practise Dharma. So putting our trust in the path is what it means to accomplish the true purpose of human life. In other words, a human birth in which we have the freedom and opportunity to practise Dharma is the karmic consequence of trusting in the path of Awakening. Such a life is rare to obtain in the first place but, once we have started to make good use of it by connecting to the path of Awakening, we will find ourselves continually born in circumstances favourable to the practice of Dharma. We only undermine the power of that connection by turning against it. As long as we still want that connection, we have it, and with it the opportunity to meet with the Dharma again and again.

Therefore, although I am personally earnestly striving to reach Awakening in this life, I am not anxious about it, because it is a great accomplishment that very few people manage. All is not lost if I fail to do so. Although it is important to aspire to reach Awakening as soon as possible, the most important thing is to trust our connection to the path of Awakening.

So there's no need, as you come to die, to be frightened by these teachings on the rarity of human birth. The last thing any Buddhist teaching is meant to do is fill people with fear at the time of death. The idea is that they make one practise to strengthen one's connection to the path of Awakening well before death, so that it's easy to face death with confidence. Whether or not we have practised much before death, all we can do is trust our connection as best we can. The instruction is always the same.

SEVEN

Calling on the power of Awakening

Turning to prayer when faced with death

In this chapter I'm going to introduce the reader to some specific practices for use at the time of death, both as examples and as suggestions for those already familiar with these practices who want to know how they fit in the general scheme of things as presented in this book. Before discussing specific practices, however, I want to familiarize the reader with the Buddhist perspective on prayer.

Even people who do not think of themselves as religious, find to their amazement that when faced with death, whether their own or that of another, they suddenly not only want to call on some higher power, but actually start to do so, even without understanding what they mean by it. They might even start praying to go to a better place or another world where they will find help and guidance.

Our strictly rational, secular, materialist, and scientific side might be saying this is just a sign of weakness, a kind of cop-out. It is just wishful thinking to want, suddenly, at the eleventh hour, to commend our spirit to some other power and be taken straight to heaven.

Of course we are right to be suspicious of a sudden recourse to blind faith in something just because we are frightened, but a sudden change of heart like this is not necessarily negative. It might even be giving in to a deeper way of knowing that we have resisted all our life, which suddenly comes alive in our hour of need. Even if the change of heart is not all that sincere, it might not be entirely negative. At the very least it might lessen our tendency to panic and open us to a certain amount of help from outside.

I don't find it surprising that this kind of thing happens. In life we tend to think we can rely on our intellect and somehow keep control of our lives and our emotions. In the face of death, we suddenly feel the rug pulled out from beneath us. The rigid logic of our intellect is no use to us in this situation, and our usual ways of keeping control fall apart. We are torn apart, worse than naked, hanging there in shock and confusion, with nowhere to turn. This is when the intuitive sense that we are not alone kicks in, and we may find ourselves linking into an intuitive sense that there is more to life than we thought and we are going to have to rely on some other power, not just ourselves.

Calling on a higher power could actually be a way of linking into the heart. This is because when we call on that power we do so from the heart. We use the phrases 'I open my heart in prayer' or 'I open my heart and call to you'. As we do this we have to let go of our egocentricity and just open to a power that can help us. What we open out to at that time is important. From the Buddhist perspective, the universe is teeming with many worlds and different kinds of beings, not all of whom are benign. Even among those who would want to help us, only those connected to the path of Awakening can actually lead us to Awakening. Even great and powerful gods are still trapped in saṃsāra. So it is important that as we open our hearts and pray, we remember it is our trust in our connection to the path of Awakening that really matters.

We can open out and try to pray to the Buddha, to Awakened beings in general, or to the Dharma, or Awakening itself, even if it is only for a moment. We can say something like, 'I don't know if you are there or not, but I am opening to you, so you must help me all you can.' We can do that even if we are full of doubts as we do so. The doubts are thoughts that come and go. The fear of not being heard is a feeling of some kind. By just opening up and praying, in spite of doubts, we can sometimes realize that we do have an intuitive sense of what it means to pray and, as we do it, some deeper understanding of the nature of reality starts to come alive in us. So it's worth giving it a go from time to time, without too much hope or expectation.

Personal and impersonal prayer

Although I have so far talked in terms of the Dharma (both as the path of Awakening and as the true nature of reality) having a protective power at the time of death, I have mostly referred to this rather impersonally, such as a power inherent in the nature of the universe. Even to call it the power of the Awakened Heart is impersonal, in the sense that it doesn't refer to a specific person. In this chapter I will continue talking about invoking an impersonal higher power, but also introduce more strongly the idea of praying to Awakened beings as actual persons.

I have avoided emphasizing this possibility before now in order to accommodate the reader who has not taken on board the Buddhist world-view. For such a reader it is already quite an intuitive leap to move from working with their direct experience in meditation to learning to trust what they are discovering in terms of its having a power from its own side. It takes yet another intuitive leap to relate to the idea that this power could manifest as specific Awakened beings to whom we could relate in a personal way.

In order to understand a whole range of practices and customs within the Buddhist tradition that relate strongly to this sense of calling on a personal other power, it is necessary to take on board the idea that, from the Buddhist perspective, Awakened beings can and do have power and influence over what happens to us, even without walking this earth as flesh and blood. This obviously suggests that they could help us just as much as we die and afterwards.

From the Buddhist perspective, there is no rigid distinction between relying on the power of our connection to the Dharma in either personal or impersonal terms. One person might open their heart at death and trust in the power of their connection to the path of Awakening, while another might open their heart and trust in the Buddha or a personal teacher to protect them. The two approaches amount to the same thing. Their effectiveness will depend on genuine openness to the true nature of reality.

As a Buddhist teacher I find I generally deal with two different kinds of people. There are those who have turned to Buddhism because they do not relate to what they think of as religious beliefs and want to rely on experiential and somewhat impersonal ways of expressing the true nature of reality. For them it is a surprise that the universe turns out to have so much heart, but they learn to relate to that as their understanding deepens. By this means they learn to trust their connection to the path of Awakening. The other kind of person has a strong intuitive sense of meaning associated with religious practices of prayer and devotion to some higher power, is typically comfortable with thinking of this as praying to actual Awakened beings, and finds the way this is explained in Buddhism helps them open their hearts and trust their connection to the power of Awakening. Some of this group feel immediately at home with Buddhist forms of devotional practice in all its elaborate detail, while others want to pray to Awakened beings, but find the style of the Buddhist practices from India and Tibet off-putting.

It is not important whether you are more comfortable with emphasizing the personal or the impersonal ways of thinking of the power of Awakening. Both are equally effective ways to pray. This power is actually beyond our limited ideas, it doesn't fit our usual idea of impersonal and personal. Our idea of a person tends to be too crude, like the limited way we think of ourselves, and our idea of an impersonal power tends to lack heart.

Therefore, in Buddhism, the line between the personal and the impersonal is not fixed and rigid. From the perspective of the Mahāyāna tradition, what we tend to think of as impersonal forces of the universe are no other than the true nature of awareness itself. From this point of view, the universe is made up of what pertains to a person and nothing else. In other words, there is no impersonal universe outside of that. Perhaps it is an intuitive sense of this that has led human beings to call on the gods of the sky, earth, and sea.

From the perspective of Mahāyāna Buddhism, an impersonal approach to prayer is more or less equivalent to relating strongly to the Buddha's non-manifest body of truth (*Dharmakāya*), whereas a personal approach is equivalent to relating to the Buddha's form body appearing to us as a particular person. Since ultimately there is no separation between the manifest and non-manifest aspects of the Buddha, it makes little difference whether we rely more on one aspect than the other. Best of all is to have a sense of both aspects at once, as when we rest in the essence of our heart. It is obviously intensely personal, and yet impersonal in the sense that it remains the same, even when all the trappings of our life and personality are stripped away from it at death.

For example, even if we are praying to the Buddha as someone who could appear to us as a person with a body, that body would be a magical apparition emanating from a deeper reality which is beyond form. We don't need to think that the Buddha's form body is fixed in a particular shape or constrained by considerations of time and place.

At death, whether we trust our connection to the path in a personal or an impersonal way, the effect of our practice is the same, in that we are opening our heart and letting go of all egocentric effort to make things happen in a particular way. Either way, we are allowing the power of the true nature of reality to respond to our need at that time by opening ourselves up to it.

This play between personal and impersonal approaches to prayer is perfectly traditional. The first thing my Tibetan friends would say to me on my deathbed would probably be 'Pray to the guru and don't worry.' This is not the place to go into what that means in detail, but essentially they would be telling me to call on the power of Awakening. In the West we often think that 'guru' refers only to a human Dharma teacher, but it's meaning is actually much subtler: it is used in Buddhism as a general term for the power of Awakening, however that reaches us. That is why my Tibetan friends would so confidently encourage me to pray in that way, even if they had no idea who my personal teacher was, or even if I had one.

The question as to what 'prayer' means naturally arises in this context. Buddhism has the idea of a wordless prayer or a prayer that goes beyond thought, just as the other great world religions. Ultimately, that is what true meditation is. However, to pray in this way is a tall order. It implies we have a completely pure and open heart. The question is, therefore, how to pray from where we are now.

In Mahāyāna Buddhism the various different aspects of prayer are summed up as seven branches. I will list them briefly to give the reader a sense of what they are. Invocation and greeting, offering and praise, asking forgiveness of wrongdoing, rejoicing in the good done by others, asking for teaching, asking the Buddhas to remain with us, and dedicating the goodness of our prayers to the Awakening of all beings. At the time of death one could take any of these aspects and use it to strengthen one's connection to the path of Awakening.

How can Awakened beings help us at death?

A few words are needed here concerning what it means to be an Awakened being. What does it mean to think of the power of the Dharma coming to us through a specific Awakened being? How is it possible to invoke them, and how can they help us at death?

I should note that, while there are different degrees of Awakening or Enlightenment, when I discuss Awakened beings and their power to help us, I am mostly thinking of Buddhas and beings close to Buddhahood, beings with immense powers and such deep wisdom that they are not bound by time and space.

In all forms of Buddhism it is understood that anyone who has reached some level of Awakening is somehow possessed of spiritual power, or adhiṣṭhāna. When we open our hearts to Awakened beings we are opening to their adhiṣṭhāna. Since the adhiṣṭhāna is essentially the power of that Awakened being's true nature (Openness, Clarity, and Sensitivity), it can connect to our true nature and influence it directly.

When we pray, or make any kind of movement in the direction of Awakening, we are linking the living truth within us, our true nature, to that of all Awakened beings. In other words, we link our essence of Openness, Clarity, and Sensitivity to their essence. Our hearts meet; we meet in our hearts. We pray because something essential to our being has been touched and is activated to respond in prayer. This movement on our part moves the heart of all Awakened beings and activates a spontaneous response.

They have made limitless praṇidhānas in the past to enable them to help us when we call for help, by removing obstacles, granting our wishes, and connecting us to the Dharma and themselves so that they can draw us to Awakening. Not only have they made these praṇidhānas in the past, but through the power of having followed the path themselves, they now have the adhiṣṭhāna to bring them to fulfilment.

Any positive actions of body, speech, and mind that we engage in generate puṇya, a power of goodness, that serves to keep adhiṣṭhāna flowing and increase its effectiveness. All the Buddhist customs concerning how to pray to Awakened beings at the time of death relate to the four principles of adhiṣṭhāna (blessing), praṇidhāna (resolves), connection, and puṇya (power of goodness, merit). As we pray to Awakened beings at death we receive their adhiṣṭhāna, we link into the power of their praṇidhānas, we strengthen our connection with the path of Awakening, and we generate puṇya that enables us to enjoy the results of our good actions.

I have expressed all this in a somewhat impersonal way. There is no mention here about the Awakened being actually being aware of our cries for help and responding from their hearts. Yet Buddhist prayers are said in just as personal a way as the prayers of any other religion. Buddhist prayers typically call on Awakened beings with words such as, 'please think of me,' 'please do not abandon me,' 'please respond to my pleas for help.' This is not because Awakened beings need persuasion to help us, but because, until we recognize our need for help, we do not sufficiently open ourselves to it. It is as if all the Awakened beings in the universe are hammering on our door trying to get in to help us, but we won't open up. We sit disgruntled behind our locked door complaining that Awakened beings never come to us, when all the time the key to opening the door lies in our hand.

There are stories of people calling to Awakened beings when they are in danger or dying, and their actually appearing before them so that they can talk to them. In other stories their presence is felt perhaps as light, or an intuitive sense of well-being. Sometimes the play of events around the dying person seems extraordinary and too precisely timed to be accidental, which from a Buddhist perspective indicates that the power of Awakened beings is at work.

It doesn't matter whether we pray with the idea that a specific Awakened being or Dharma teacher is with us, or with the idea that all those who are Awakened are naturally present everywhere. From a very deep perspective, one could say that the world of every specific Awakened being interpenetrates the worlds of all other Awakened beings, so that to call on one is to call on all. By the same token, to call on them all is to call on every one. One could argue that, practically speaking, it is easier to focus on one rather than all, and there is much to be learned from focusing on one, that will then apply to all. It is a matter of following one's heart in this respect and praying in whatever way you find gives you most confidence and conviction.

In the light of this background of Buddhist ideas about the nature of Awakened beings and how they can help us at death, I will now describe some actual practices that someone following the path to Awakening might rely on.

Refuge and Bodhisattva vows

In the Introduction I mentioned that Buddhists take Refuge in the Three Jewels. There is no better protection at death than the Refuge vow that one takes on becoming a Buddhist. We make the Refuge vow with our whole heart, committing ourselves with conviction to the path of Awakening. We call on all the Buddhas to be our witnesses in order to strengthen our heart connection with them.

Once we have committed ourselves in this way, that commitment is always with us, even when we are not thinking about it, and it acts as a protection in its own right. It prevents us from straying into states of mind opposed to that commitment. Because of that commitment, as soon as we start to stray we feel uneasy, and that tends to draw us back to the path. From the Buddhist point of view, commitments made in one life are like seeds that ripen as a natural tendency to keep to those same commitments in a future life, even though one no longer remembers having made the commitment. The commitment has a kind of power that is not interrupted by what happens at death.

Although going for Refuge is a big topic in its own right, anyone who is familiar with the Buddhist tradition will know that reciting the words, 'I go for Refuge in the Buddha, I go for Refuge in the Dharma, I go for Refuge in the Sangha,' is a practice in itself. To keep repeating these words at the time of death would be an excellent way to go. Reciting these words is thought of as having power in its own right. When recited with a deep trust in one's connection to the path of Awakening, this would be a complete practice in itself.

By reciting the Refuges in this way, one is bringing the Dharma to mind again and again, one is reinforcing one's resolve to follow the Dharma, one is accumulating puṇya. Furthermore, one is opening to the adhiṣṭhāna of the Three Jewels, and if one recites the Refuges with an open and trusting heart, one is connecting directly to the true nature of reality within oneself and all beings.

The Bodhisattva vow is the vow to bring all beings to Awakening. It is an extension of the Refuge vow. To be committed to Awakening all beings is to have taken Refuge in the Three Jewels; having taken Refuge in the Three Jewels, one will eventually find oneself working to bring all beings to Awakening.

For those who have taken the Bodhisattva vow as well as the Refuge vow, simply reciting a formulation of that vow would be sufficient practice itself. The benefits of reciting the Bodhisattva vow are the same as those of reciting the Refuges. The difference is only in how deeply we understand what we are committing ourselves to. For example, one could recite the words, 'I will never abandon the path to Awakening until all beings reach complete Enlightenment,' or 'just as beings are without limit, so my commitment to save them all is without limit. I will not abandon any living being until all attain Enlightenment.'

For a person who has taken this vow, especially if they have taken it formally from a teacher, remembering this as they die is sufficient practice in itself. It expresses itself in their whole way of being and will naturally keep them connected to the path, however difficult their death process turns out to be.

Invoking Awakened beings

If you find the idea of invoking Awakened beings inspiring, you may find it helpful to invoke such a presence into the vastness of space before you, in the form of whatever Awakened being you feel the strongest connection with. You might want to think of that Awakened being appearing in a blaze of glory, surrounded by his or her whole world filled with other beings, all rejoicing and sending out light into the world and to you, to remove obscurations, obstacles, hindrances, sickness, dangers, and bring down a rain of all manner of good things. Rather than imagining all this in detail, you might prefer to imagine basking in the light of all this, perhaps a golden or rainbow light. The important thing is to open out into the possibility that such a thing could happen. From the point of view of Awakened beings, this is happening all the time; it is our lack of openness that prevents us feeling the benefit of it.

It can be a powerful practice to think of the power of Awakening in this somewhat personal way, thinking that the being or beings, whose presence you feel, are the embodiment of the truth, wisdom, and compassion of all Awakened beings. You may find that thinking like this allows you to open your heart to their presence with love and trust more easily.

When praying to an Awakened being, some people find that not only does it help to visualize the being in empty space before them, but also to imagine them smiling with love and compassion, forgiving all misdeeds, doubts, and weaknesses. Their adhiṣṭhāna can be visualized in the form of light streaming from their heart to your own heart, removing sickness, obscurations, and negativity, giving you spiritual strength and drawing you to them. Having done this you may find you feel totally immersed in light, as if all your suffering and negativity has been completely dissolved or washed away by the power of the presence of the light before you. If this happens, just rest in that sense of freedom and being really in touch with your true nature, the Awakened Heart.

Whether you visualize Awakened beings in this way or simply open your heart and feel their presence and their love and adhiṣṭhāna coming to you, the benefits are the same. If this is done in the same spirit as reciting the Refuge or Bodhisattva vows, the benefits of doing it are the same. Visualizing the presence of Awakened beings as one recites prayers and praṇidhānas is a way of feeling their presence more tangibly. Sometimes one can feel that presence more tangibly by not visualizing, so the important thing is to do what most naturally increases your confidence and conviction and helps you trust your connection to the path of Awakening.

Mantras or names of the Buddha

As well as, or instead of, reciting the Refuge and Bodhisattva vows or visualizing the presence of Awakened beings, you could invoke the presence of Awakened beings simply by reciting a mantra or the name of a Buddha. For example, one could recite the Perfection of Wisdom mantra, *'oṃ gate gate pāragate pārasaṃgate bodhi svāhā'*; the Buddha's mantra, *'oṃ muni muni mahāmuni śakyāmunaye svāhā'*; the Guru Rinpoche (Padmasambhava, the Lotus Born) mantra, *'oṃ āḥ hūṃ vajra guru padma siddhi hūṃ'*; the Avalokiteśvara (the embodiment of compassion in male form) mantra, *'oṃ maṇi padme hūṃ'*, or the Tārā (the embodiment of compassion in female form) mantra, *'oṃ tāre tuttāre ture svāhā'*; or simply recite, *'Buddha, Buddha, Buddha'*.

The benefits of reciting mantras and the names of Buddhas are the same. According to the Buddhist tradition, they have a tremendous adhiṣṭhāna, from their own side, independent of us. Both the names of Buddhas and their mantras emanate from the heart of Awakened beings, they embody the Awakened Heart, so by reciting them we link directly into the Heart of Awakening. If we receive the name or mantra from an accomplished practitioner who is strongly connected to the Awakened Being from which the mantra emanates, that creates a special link for us to that being. So it is good to get it from a reliable source. But the most important thing is to recite it with a sense of trust in our connection to the path of Awakening.

Not everyone relates to mantras very well, while others find it easier to relate to a mantra than to any other practice. People often find it is easier to recite mantras than to meditate, especially when they feel unwell or overcome with emotion. If you have already established a connection with mantra recitation and find it easier to link into this than some other meditation practice, follow your inclination. The important thing at death is feel confident in your connection with the heart of Awakening in whatever way comes to you most naturally.

Some people find the mantra takes off by itself and they can feel it going on all the time whether or not they are focusing on it. This acts as a constant reminder of the presence of the truth of Awakening; it serves as an anchor and protection for the mind. It is a very immediate way of linking into the heart and feeling connected to the essence of Awakening.

Whether one relates to mantras or not seems to depend on the kind of connections one has made with the path of Awakening in past lives. A combination of sometimes reciting mantras, sometimes the names of Buddha, and sometimes Refuge and Bodhisattva vows, would be a way of bringing to mind all the different aspects of what it means to trust our connection to the path of Awakening. The more you can sense the presence of Awakened beings, or one's teachers or Dharma friends, the better. And if visualizing them helps increase the sense of their presence, do it again and again.

Sometimes, simply stop and meditate by resting in the heart and opening out into space, just letting whatever experience is arising be as it is, without trying to stop it or letting yourself get lost in it.

Praying to be born in a Pure Land

Every Awakened being exists in their own Awakened world, often called a Pure Land, and is able to draw us into that world when we call on them, especially at the time of death. Having created their own Pure Land through the power of their praṇidhānas over countless lifetimes, they are able to draw into it any being who thinks of them or calls to them at the time of death, and hold them there until they reach Awakening.

Buddhist teachings on Pure Lands constitute a vast topic. There are many kinds of Pure Land and a lot of technical detail and principles involved. But even without knowing much about them, someone can have a sense that it would be wonderful to be born into the presence of a particular Awakened being, and aspire to be born into their Pure Land. Pure Lands are always spoken of as being in the heart as well as being real places where you can go and live. This is not a completely unfamiliar idea to us. We sometimes talk poetically not only of having our dearest friends in our heart, but also of places that are dear to us seeming to be in our heart and our heart seeming to be there even when we are far away.

At death, we often find people talking about passing over to the other side, another place, a better place, the other world, or the hereafter, even when they have no specific beliefs in this regard. It is as if people intuitively sense that a person and their world are all of a piece. Where they are, their world will be too. So it is not such a big intuitive leap to think of Awakened beings living in their own worlds into which we could pray to be reborn.

In Tibetan, Chinese, and Japanese Buddhism, a popular practice is praying to be born in Amitābha's Pure Land, Sukhāvati

(Tibetan *Dewachen*, meaning Land of Great Bliss). Some people make this their main practice, while others combine it with other practices such as those I have outlined. The practice essentially consists in reciting the name of Amitābha Buddha (Amitābha means Boundless Light – Amida in the Japanese tradition) and perhaps also his mantra, or that of Avalokiteśvara, together with a prayer such as, 'As soon as I die, may I see the Buddha Amitābha and be born in the land of Sukhāvati. Having been born there, may I complete the path to Awakening and bring all beings to Awakening with me.'

As we utter the name or mantra of an Awakened being, or even the name of their Pure Land, we are automatically making a connection with the world emanating from that being, and that naturally draws us towards it by the force of its adhiṣṭhāna.

Every fully Awakened being has a Pure Land, and they are equally conducive to Awakening. It doesn't really matter which one you choose and whether you focus on the Pure Land or just the Awakened Heart of the Awakened being you have chosen. Once you have been born in one Pure Land it is easy to travel to another, so it doesn't matter much which one you focus on. Some people are determined to go to one particular Pure Land. That is one way of practising that can be quite energizing. Because Guru Rinpoche is central to the Mahāmudrā and Dzogchen tradition, I encourage my students to feel a strong connection with him as one of the great living forces of Tibetan Buddhism. Since Guru Rinpoche emanates from Amitābha, calling on him opens the way to Sukhāvati as well as Guru Rinpoche's personal Pure Land. It is said that Guru Rinpoche was specially sent by the Buddha Amitābha to help the beings of this 'dark age' when it is very hard to practise Dharma.

Other people find they do not favour one Pure Land or Awakened being over another, and are happy to think of them all as the same in essence and relate to the essence of them all. This would be more like someone who relied mainly on the Refuge or

Bodhisattva vow or meditation as their main practice at the time of death. The benefits of all these practices are the same.

When praying to be reborn in a Pure Land the idea is simply to have faith in the Buddha whose land it is and not make any ego-centric effort to *do* anything oneself, except recite the mantra or prayer to be born in that land. The recitation is done with complete trust that maintaining the connection is sufficient and that the Buddha will do the rest. It is a way of letting go of attachment to egocentric ideas of self-effort and to trust our heart connection to the Buddha to do all the work of Awakening the heart within us. In that sense it works like meditation, and it is very good to combine sessions of meditation with sessions of prayer and trusting in Amitābha or whichever Awakened being you have chosen.

To die with such a longing is the same as dying with the longing to be able to realize full Awakening in order to benefit all beings. Thinking in terms of taking birth in a Pure Land gives the practice a personal touch. To help you feel more confident in your connection to the path of Awakening, you could think of the warmth and love of Awakened beings coming towards you to embrace you and escort you to their Pure Land.

Powa, the transference of consciousness
A special way of opening out with trust in the path of Awakening is a practice called *powa* in Tibetan. *Powa* means 'transference' and is a special method for transferring oneself or another being from this body and life directly into either a state of Awakening or a Pure Land without having to go through the intermediate state. It uses all the elements mentioned so far, such as the power of adhiṣṭhāna, praṇidhānas, connections, puṇya, mantra, prayer, and meditation. The benefits of the powa practice are the same as for all the above practices.

There are different kinds of powa practice. Some involve the use of a lot of imagery and visualization. Among Tibetans, powa is practised mainly in order to take birth in Amitābha's Pure Land, so the practice involves many recitations of Amitābha's mantra and prayers to Amitābha and praṇidhānas to be born in his Pure Land.

Some practitioners specialize in powa practice and are able to effectively help others pass quickly from this world to Amitābha's Pure Land by meditating alongside a person as they die and getting their consciousness to depart from the body through the crown of the head. It is said that the force of concentration on the part of the meditator and the person being helped produces a hole as the consciousness leaves the body. It is rather impressive to see a stalk of grass sticking out of a hole in a skull, which is put there as evidence that the powa was successful.

If powa is being done for you by someone else, it is ideally done in your presence at the exact moment of death. It can also be done a little before, or even long after, the person dies. There are a lot of technicalities involved in this practice, so only an expert knows exactly how and when to do it to best effect.

There is not much point in trying to learn elaborate powa practices from a book without a living connection with a lineage of advanced practitioners who have the power to transmit the essence of the practice. Furthermore, the more elaborate forms of the practice can be dangerous without expert supervision. However, there are simpler forms of powa that you can practise, for yourself or for others, even if you do not have the transmission or supervision for a more elaborate version.

Sogyal Rinpoche's *Tibetan Book of Living and Dying* describes three kinds of powa practice that anyone can do, Buddhist or not. The first two are like the practices on how to invoke Awakened beings by prayer, visualization, and mantra. As well as feeling the presence of Awakened beings and thinking of their adhiṣṭhāna entering us, in the powa practice one imagines that one's consciousness leaves the body and melts directly into the heart of the Awakened being in the sky in front of one.

The third practice is called the most essential powa practice. This is very close to the kind of practice I have been recommending throughout this book. The additional element is simply to say 'Ah!', with complete confidence that our heart, the heart of the Buddha, and the hearts of all beings, are of one essence. All beings are in our heart, and the deceased is in our heart, and our heart is in the heart of the Buddha. Thinking like this and trusting our connection to the path of Awakening, we just relax all clinging and, with a sense of relief and wonder, utter 'Ah!'. It is good to do this as often as you think of it, remembering Natsok Rangdröl's remark that even a few moments of recognition of our true nature is enough to liberate us when we are in the intermediate state.

The simple form of the most essential powa practice given here can be done before, during, and after death. Having said 'Ah!' a few times, rest in meditation, trusting that your heart and the hearts of all Awakened beings are naturally inseparable and interpenetrating in the Openness, Clarity, and Sensitivity of our being. Let go of doubts and hesitations and any other thoughts that appear in the mind, and rest in what is beyond all concepts of space and time. This means resting in not knowing anything, being nowhere, ungraspable and yet all-pervading, the essence of all beings. Resting like this in meditation helps hold you in a stable and safe place in which you will be able to recover yourself and move on with courage and reassurance.

If you are doing this essential powa practice on behalf of another person, think that their heart is inseparable from yours and that of all Awakened beings as you do it.

As presented here, powa might appear a simple and perhaps even elementary practice, but it is extremely profound. In order to connect to the full power of the adhiṣṭhāna of the powa practice, one needs the live transmission and instruction from an experienced practitioner. Without this kind of connection it would be like having an electric appliance dicconnected from any effective power source. That is not to say that there is any harm in trying. Awakened beings are always present, so if we can open, who can say what might be possible?

So I think it is worth mentioning the powa, especially the essential powa practice, in a general way, in case someone reading is inspired by it and thereby given confidence as they die, even without having had the full instruction and transmission. Profound practices can sometimes work quite spontaneously, seemingly without any elaborate preparation. Maybe that is because the person concerned has a connection with that practice from past lives.

Follow your own inspiration

Some people find the idea of Awakened beings and Pure Lands inspiring, but it probably sounds fanciful to many more. These ideas imply all sorts of things about the nature of the universe that might be hard for us to relate to. At this stage we have to accept on trust, since we do not understand things in that way, at least not yet. From the Buddhist perspective, that is because our vision is too obscured by our strongly held beliefs about what reality really is.

Meditation is the way to remove these obscurations. That is why I put so much emphasis on meditation. Since meditation is about our direct experience and does not require us to accept any belief system, it is the way in for everyone and also the way forward in terms of deepening our understanding. The benefits of meditation and having the right attitudes at the time of death are the same as doing any of the practices mentioned in this book. Meditation has its own adhiṣṭhāna and connects directly to the true nature of reality, the source of all power. As always, it is for us to choose which practice we want to rely on at the time of death to keep us connected to the path of Awakening.

So what makes us choose one practice rather than another? Why choose one Awakened being rather than another? Why choose to be born in one Pure Land rather than another? I find it quite mysterious how people relate differently to things. The Buddhist view on this is that we choose according to our karmic propensities in this and past lives, our connections now, and from past lives, and praṇidhānas we make now and have made in past lives.

EIGHT

How the living can help the dead or dying

In this chapter, I will draw together various suggestions that relate to helping others as they die and after their death. This includes suggestions on how to care for both Buddhists and non-Buddhists, the actual person dying, as well as those who are close to them.

Being with the dying

The vital point to remember is just to be there for the other person without being anxious about whether or not one is doing the right thing. Often just the presence of someone who cares, and who isn't in a hurry to rush away, can somehow restore faith in oneself, faith that one is somehow connected with others at a deep level. That can be a tremendous help. So staying with a dying person, and letting them feel you are there for them, can already communicate a lot. It also gives them an opportunity to tell you what they are thinking, if that is what they want to do. Staying beside them in a relaxed way, it is likely to become obvious whether they want input from you. So it's a matter of being as open, clear, and sensitive as you can.

When we get anxious, we tend to miss opportunities to respond to what the dying person wants or is trying to communicate. Maybe their greatest fear is feeling abandoned and alone. All they need is for you to be there. If you are anxious, you might start jumping up and down and rushing around doing things in a way that makes them feel abandoned and ignored. Obviously one has to take one's cue from the dying person about what their particular needs are at that moment. You have to keep awake and use your intelligence or intuition about what is needed.

Being there with someone doesn't necessarily feel comfortable. Sometimes you can't tell whether your presence is appreciated or not. I have often been surprised by people's response to my presence. Sometimes it is very positive, even when I haven't done much or I have felt I've made every mistake in the book. Somehow my intention seemed to come through regardless. At other times, in spite of my good intentions and my sense that I acted appropriately, people have not been happy with me. It is like that sometimes. We just have to do the best we can. That is all there is to it. Helping the dying is not about making us feel good about ourselves.

In a very moving article on how to be with the dying, Chögyam Trungpa Rinpoche, one of my teachers, stresses the importance of just being ordinary and down to earth, allowing the dying person to talk about whatever they wish and tuning in to their ordinary hopes and fears about life and death. This somehow makes them feel real, rather than some kind of species apart. If we are frightened by death ourselves, it is very difficult to be with a dying person in a real way like this. We tend to look at them through the veil of our own hopes and fears, rather than meet them on their own ground.

Trungpa Rinpoche also explained how it is important to stress continuity of awareness to the dying person. One of their greatest fears at death is annihilation. This is made worse by everyone acting as if they no longer existed as a real person. So talking to them in a down-to-earth kind of way reassures them that you do not think of them as about to be annihilated. This can inspire trust, because they know you believe in them and will continue to be there for them as they die.

As they go through the death process and in the intermediate state that follows, they are likely to experience many strange things which they need to relate to as simply and directly as possible. They need to recognize that whatever is appearing or happening to them is the play of their own mind, like dreams and hallucinations, and that it is useless to try to run away from them. Your being there, reassuring them, provides a stable place from which they can learn to have confidence in the continuity of their awareness. Their connection with you can help them feel grounded rather than chased here and there by rapidly changing sensations and appearances. Your gift to them is the reassurance that they are not alone and not about to be annihilated.

Giving spiritual advice to the dying

People sometimes ask me for advice on what to say to a dying person. It is not easy to generalize, since everyone is so different. You have to use your own intuition about that really.

Obviously the more aware we are of who the dying person is, and what they believe in, the easier it will be to find appropriate things to say. Although some people appreciate advice and encouragement, not everyone does. It is a matter of spotting opportunities to encourage the dying person in appropriate lines of thinking that will give them courage and confidence. This means discouraging them as much as possible from dwelling on disturbing thoughts arising from attachment, anger, and confusion.

In traditional Buddhist cultures it is customary to sit at the bedside of a dying person and recount to them their good deeds, for example, 'Remember the time when you made offerings in the temple,' 'Remember the time when you saved the life of a drowning bumble bee,' or 'Remember the kind words you said to restore harmony among quarrelling friends.' The idea is to help the person die in a positive frame of mind, confidently focused on their good deeds and reinforcing their wish to repeat them, which will hopefully propel the dying person into a positive rebirth.

In our culture, reminding people of their good deeds can be a risky proposition, as people can often be dismissive and unconvinced about the good they've done, being so fixated on the bad they have done. In my experience, we are more convinced about our ability to have good intentions and a good basic attitude right now, than about the good we have done in the past. Since that is actually the most important thing, I suggest encouraging the dying person and those around them to focus on and link into whatever positive attitude comes most naturally to them.

If you find yourself sitting not really knowing what to say, it is important not to mind that and even to say quite simply, 'I don't know what to say.' At least that is honest and open. From my own experience, I know that it is sometimes amazingly helpful just to hear someone stating the obvious very boldly and confidently. It can make me laugh!

Among the things you might find appropriate to say is that our heart – our true nature – can never be destroyed, so our heart will always be with them. In particular, it is good to reassure them. The dying person may need reassuring that they have done all they can for their loved ones in this life, and their loved ones will always be with them in their heart, so the dying person can let go of them.

It can be helpful to slip in reminders of impermanence from time to time, such as the observation that there is no point in getting attached to things, since they will all be gone once they are dead. Similarly, it can be a helpful reminder that any suffering will not last forever.

Even for those who have no belief in karma and a future life, it can still be reassuring to be reminded that they have always tried to live a good life. Being reminded of the many good things they have done is good for boosting morale, as well as for strengthening their good tendencies. If they are full of remorse at wrongs they have committed, try to reassure them that the important thing is that they are sorry and determined not to behave like that again. If they believe in future lives, you can reassure them that they will get a chance to make up when they meet again the people they wronged. The more you can get them to trust the goodness of their heart and their good intentions the better.

If the dying person's mind becomes very confused, they will need more reassurance than ever. They need reassuring that their mind will become clear again. They won't always be confused. You may find you can reassure them that it is only their mind that is confused; they are not confused in their heart.

Sometimes the dying person can be persuaded that dying is like relaxing after a hard day's work. Their task is done and tomorrow will be a new day, a new place, a new life. This might help them relax into their heart with a feeling of confidence.

It is often the case these days that one has to care for someone with no beliefs at all and they don't even want to talk about the fact they are dying, much less the question of life and death in general. Many people put a lid on this kind of thinking early in life and just don't want to think about anything to do with death. They would even like to pretend it is not happening to them. In my experience there doesn't seem much one can do about this, except hope that if there is some kind of opening on their part one will find the right thing to say. Trying to impose our own view of reality on someone else doesn't seem to help.

Of course, it is also important to find out if the dying person has any specific wishes. For example, do they need help or company? If so, what kind and whose? Would they like to talk? If so, with whom? Do they want to know the truth? Do their relatives and friends know their condition? Can you help them inform their relatives and friends? Is there anyone they want to make peace with? Have they written a will? Are their affairs in order, their debts and bills paid, dependants and pets cared for, borrowed property returned, and so on?

It might be that the dying person cannot talk for some reason, but can respond with signals of some kind. This requires some ingenuity and it is perhaps worth thinking in advance about how to phrase questions to get maximum information from yes or no answers. 'How do you feel?' might be useless, whereas 'are you feeling better?' is easy to respond to. 'Are you worried about anything?' could evoke a nod, and then you would need to suggest what their worries might be and how you might help.

Helping dying Buddhists

If the person you are caring for is a practising Buddhist, the most important thing is to find out what they have most faith in and encourage them to focus on that and to rely on their connection with that practice. All the suggestions in this book about what attitudes to adopt, trusting one's connection to the path, and calling on the power of Awakening, are relevant here. Encourage them in whatever practice they link into most easily.

As I have continually stressed, it is a person's attitude and the whole orientation of their being that has the biggest effect when they come to die. So it is more important to help people cultivate a Dharma attitude than it is to pressure them to do lots of formal Dharma practice, which they might find difficult at that time.

If the dying person is a meditator who finds they cannot meditate because of the stress, encourage them to have faith in the meditation they did in the past. They need reassuring that it doesn't matter about not meditating right then, they can resume it later. Meanwhile, they need to trust what they have done already and that their good intentions will carry them through. It is important for them not to have unrealistic expectations of themselves or castigate themselves for not being better meditators. If you offer to sit and meditate alongside them, this might actually help them link into meditation, or at least join you in spirit. At the very least, their meditation in life should have given them an underlying confidence in the nature of their experience, which should enable them to open to situations in a meditative way, even if they don't feel particularly meditative or peaceful right now.

Intention is the engine that carries us to Awakening, so it is good to encourage them to make resolves and wishes (*praṇidhānas*) for their future lives. For example, to help others, to meet the path to Awakening again, and to meet those with whom they have strong Dharma connections, and even (if they are inspired by this vision) to work for ever to bring all beings to Awakening.

More practically, you could offer to help them listen to Dharma in some form. You could play tapes, read to them, get them to read, or frame short sayings that they find inspiring and encourage them to look at them from time to time. You could place a Buddha image or picture near their head.

If the dying person wants the image at the foot of the bed where they can see it, that is fine, even though, traditionally, it is regarded as disrespectful to have your feet pointing at a Buddha. It doesn't matter much, because for us it is not regarded as disrespectful to have our feet pointing at someone. What is more, it is regarded as respectful to want to keep our eyes on someone we love. In Buddhist countries, pointing your feet at anyone is regarded as disrespectful, so if you felt like that, you would never have your feet pointing at a Buddha image. However, since we westerners don't usually think like this, we might prefer to have the image at the end of the bed. We would be thinking the image was out there above us.

If you have blessed or sacred substances or artefacts to touch the dying person with, especially on the head or heart, this is a way of strengthening their connection to the Dharma. A blessed object is one that has been linked to the praṇidhānas and the adhiṣṭhāna of Awakened beings. The idea is that blessed images, artefacts, substances, and sacred writings touched, seen, or sensed in some other way give the dying person a connection to the Dharma in a physical way that has power from its own side.

The same applies to mantras. Quietly reciting mantras might not only be quite reassuring and calming, but also add to the strength of the dying person's Dharma connections. Adhiṣṭhāna can be made to flow in this way, acting as protection and attracting favourable conditions for a happy rebirth. Some people, even though not Buddhist, are open to having things like a Buddha image near them and having mantras recited for them.

When someone loses their mind

The intense suffering, sometimes protracted, that often precedes the death experience often robs a person of their dignity, clarity, and presence of mind. When that happens, people can begin to behave quite bizarrely, regressing to past memories and traumas, hallucinating, not recognizing their loved ones or surroundings, and so on. This can be very upsetting for us as well as for them, so it is a very difficult situation.

It is important not to close off and try to put that person out of your mind. They still need our love and attention. Even if we cannot help them much by our presence, we can still keep them constantly in our hearts.

People wonder what has happened to the person they knew. Can all the good qualities they displayed throughout their life suddenly count for nothing? The Buddhist view that our Awakened Heart, with its intrinsic qualities of openness, clarity, and sensitivity, is indestructible, can be very reassuring. Even though those qualities have been temporarily occluded by the changes they are undergoing, that doesn't mean they have diminished, and from the karmic point of view the results of their previous goodness is still there waiting to ripen. Nothing is lost. After death their habitual good deeds and clarity of mind will reassert themselves. Meanwhile, you can be there for them, and pray they do not meet with any obstacles or suffer the consequences of any violent or abusive behaviour they may exhibit. From the karmic point of view, because they lack control, their actions will not bring such severe consequences as those done deliberately. Nonetheless, negative states of mind are always fuelled by confusion and lead to suffering. For someone suffering in this way, it is good to practise tonglen to give rise to compassion, and make praṇidhānas to strengthen their connection with Awakening.

Helping those losing a loved one

When we are with someone who is dying or who has died, their own loved ones often need our help as much as they do. They are likely to be anxious and confused at having to cope with a situation that they are unprepared for, especially if death is something they have never thought much about. Your example at such a time can be deeply affecting. By finding ways to relieve their distress and keep them calm and confident, you help take the pressure off the dying person, which allows them to relax and let go of attachment and worry. So keeping yourself calm and reassuring those around you can be your most important function at this time.

You might get an opportunity to say to those close to the dying person that Buddhists believe that our connection with someone who has died continues beyond death, and they can help by wishing them well on their journey and looking forward to meeting them again. Those who are left behind need to make their peace with the person who is dying as much as the dying need to make their peace with the living before it is too late. In this way they can meet in future lives on good terms. This means letting go of negativity or attachment in regard to each other, and wishing each other well with a confident and peaceful mind.

One of the worst sufferings when losing a loved one is a feeling of helplessness. Even non-Buddhists can derive great comfort from feeling they are able to do something for the person who has died, such as making gifts to charities on their behalf, or reciting praṇidhānas or mantras. Those left behind might not be sure whether they have faith in all this sort of thing, but it can still be quite reassuring to be doing things, just in case it helps. Even children can participate in this kind of thing. From the Buddhist perspective, this has a positive effect regardless of whether they believe in what they are doing.

Around the moment of death

There are various physical things one might do for a dying person, such as holding their hand or gently holding or massaging them. However, according to the Buddhist tradition, as the moment of death approaches it is generally best not to touch or move the body in order not to disturb the process. It is said that, if the dying person's attention is drawn to the lower part of their body, this can create a connection that draws them into a less than favourable rebirth. This is obviously a very mysterious idea, and there is not much I can say here to explain it. It relates to a view of mind and body that are very different to our usual one.

Since the mind is more important than the body, if to let go of the dying person's hand will distress them, it is more important to hold it as long as they want. If the dying person doesn't seem particularly bothered by your letting go their hand, it is best to let go as the actual moment of death approaches. It is the heart connection that is most important at that time, so we should rely on that and trust it. Since the dying person's body is deteriorating and becoming useless to them, we do not want to encourage attachment to it but get them to rest in their heart as much as possible.

According to the Buddhist tradition, if the dying person's attention moves up towards their head, this may ease their progress towards a favourable rebirth. Therefore, at the very last, you might try to place yourself behind or near their head in order to attract their attention upwards as they die.

Right at the very end, when you know for sure they are about to die, whisper very quietly to them that they are dying and tell them to relax and not be afraid. It is said that on the brink of death, even if a person seems to have already slipped into unconsciousness, it is possible they can still hear and might even have a heightened sensitivity to sound. That is why it's important to speak quietly as a person is dying, and to avoid loud noise.

It can be very disturbing for a dying person to have dear ones lamenting and begging them not to die. This is hard because sometimes, when the outcome lies in the balance, it is the connection with loved ones that helps people pull through and they don't die. We need to be ready for that difficult point of transition when it is clear there is no more hope. In the end, the dying person needs reassurance that it is all right to die. It is normal. It is not letting anyone down. So, as soon as it is clear that the person really is dying, it is better for all lamentation to cease and everyone concerned to give up attachment and let them die in peace.

Talking to the dead

According to Buddhist teachings, once we have left the body and are in the intermediate state before rebirth, we float freely and no longer suffer the physical limitations that prevent our knowing what others are thinking, and we are able to go anywhere we think of. In other words, we just go to wherever we think of, and we know what is going on there. If you think how quickly and easily the mind moves, it is easy to understand how unstable and unsettling must be the experience of the intermediate state. So if a dead person thinks of us, it would be very helpful for them if we were thinking about them in a reassuring and helpful way. Therefore it is important to think well of them immediately after they die.

It is also taught that the dead person in the intermediate state often doesn't realize they have died, so they hang around their home and old haunts as if they were still alive. They can feel unhappy, and even angry, to see people taking over their home and possessions. So it is helpful to keep talking to them and telling them they have died, and that no offence is meant. This is particularly helpful in the case of a violent or sudden death, in which case, if possible, we talk to them at the place where they have died or where their body is.

This can be done mentally or even out loud, telling them that they are dead and giving them good Dharma advice about not being afraid, letting go of attachment, not getting angry, trusting their deepest heart wish for happiness and truth, in whatever terms you think they will understand. If they were Buddhist, remind them of the path to Awakening, Awakened beings, or whatever teaching or practice they had confidence in. If they were not Buddhist, but very kind and compassionate, remind them how this will protect them and that they should continue to trust that way of being and let it guide them.

Since it is believed that the being in the intermediate state has the power of knowing what others are thinking, it is very important to take special care of your thoughts and emotions at the time of a person's death. Of course we cannot help having negative thoughts and emotions, but we can have a good attitude towards them, regretting the negative ones and fostering the positive ones, without clinging on to any of them, just recognizing thoughts are thoughts. This will help the dead person do the same.

Practising to benefit the dying or deceased
When someone is dying, and after they have died, is a specially good time to do Dharma practice and dedicate it for their benefit. Your practice at this time can really benefit them, in a way that goes beyond the psychological level of helping them be calm or have a good attitude as they are dying.

Whatever Dharma practice you do can be a comfort to the deceased person in the intermediate state, even if it is just the way you think about the Dharma as you go about your daily life. The deceased is likely to be going through a time of great turmoil and confusion, not knowing where they are, where they are going, or what is going to happen next, so your calmness and clarity, full of love and concern, provide a stable place in which they can find peace and the courage to face whatever is happening to them. It helps them to turn their own hearts and minds in the direction of truth and Awakening.

As I said earlier, the consciousness in the intermediate state after death is very volatile, and possessed of rudimentary clairvoyance. So if you practise Dharma, the deceased person can strongly link into that, probably much more than in life. They might suddenly understand why you practise Dharma. It could even provide a positive connection for them that might lead them directly to a favourable rebirth. Of course, it all depends on the person and their karma, but these possibilities really exist. We can even help people who have died years and years ago because time (in the way we think of it) is not ultimately real. So we need never feel that it is too late.

Our Dharma practice makes a connection with Awakening for the deceased person, through their connection with us. This is because heart connections are real and our heart has been touched by them. That connection is inescapable and will draw them into our world, and our world is intimately connected to Awakening. The stronger their connection with us, the more powerful this can be. But even simply to have heard someone's name, or to have been part of a shared world (as when we hear about disasters) forms a connection with us and thus with Awakening (since we are connected to the path of Awakening). If we dedicate our practice to those who have died, thinking of them as we do so, it helps make that connection stronger. It doesn't matter whether the person believes in these connections or not; from the Buddhist perspective they are real and are a conduit for help to reach us.

The simplest way to help others who have died is to dedicate our regular Dharma practice to them, mentioning them by name. I keep a list of people who have recently died or who are in trouble, and when we are on retreat, I and my students read this list out at the end of the day. We dedicate our Dharma practice to the Awakening of all sentient beings, but especially to those people.

Obviously, as we do Dharma practices for the deceased, we try to be as present and as genuine as we can, but it is natural to experience all sorts of doubts and wonder if we are doing enough. We have two options at this point. Either we decide to let such thoughts inspire us enthusiastically to do more, or we decide to treat them like any other thoughts that come and go. The important thing is to remain as relaxed, confident, and simple as you can. Don't be hard on yourself for having doubts and strong emotions.

Because we are likely to feel very disturbed at the time of a person's death, and we may be very aware how disturbed they were, or are, as well as the people around them, it helps to remember that Dharma practice has power from its own side. It helps the deceased in a way that is deeper than a mere psychological level. The power of the practice comes from the true nature of reality and from the power of our heart connection with the true nature of reality. So the most important thing is to rest in the heart and not to worry.

Typical traditional Buddhist customs

In Buddhist countries people often like to do a large number of things on behalf of the dead. There are many options and it is very much up to individuals what they choose to do as a practice for the deceased. A lot depends on their relationship to them and what inspires them at the time.

For example, it is common for the whole family to go to a shrine, holy place, or monastery and offer gifts such as candles, flowers, incense, and even large sums of money, on behalf of the deceased, to the Buddha, Dharma, and Sangha. Sometimes they offer hundreds or thousands of candles or butter lamps, or a meal for a whole monastery or community of practitioners, or money to as many Dharma practitioners and teachers as they can. This is another way of making connections for the deceased to link them to path of Awakening. As they make these offerings they ask teachers and practitioners to protect the deceased by the adhiṣṭhāna of their wisdom and compassion. They might ask a whole monastery, or maybe several monasteries and high-ranking teachers, such as the Dalai Lama, to pray for them, making lots of offerings every time they ask.

Other practices might include reciting prayers or scriptures for several days or weeks on end, taking a vow of abstinence, going on pilgrimage, and so on. The idea is to accumulate puṇya and bring together as many conditions as possible to help the deceased face the dangers in the intermediate state, and to find a favourable rebirth, as well as create auspicious situations and connections with Awakening for that person for all their future lives.

How much Dharma practice should I do?
People often want to know how much practice to do and for how long. It's not really possible to answer such a question. Obviously as much as possible is good, but there has to be some kind of limit. Maybe the best guide is to do as much as you can with enthusiasm. At a certain point, we feel it is time to get on with attending to the rest of our life. I find it helpful to maintain a balance between the general good of all beings (which includes the deceased) and the specific case of the deceased. Sometimes I simply do my regular practice while thinking that my heart, the heart of the deceased, and the heart of all Awakened beings are inseparable, and then dedicate the practice with a praṇidhāna for the Awakening of all beings, making special reference to the

deceased. Sometimes I feel inspired to do extra prayers or practices for particular people that I feel I have strong connection with.

In the Tibetan Buddhist tradition, the custom is to do special practices for the deceased for seven weeks (forty-nine days) after they have died. Generally speaking, though, the timing is more important for the living than the dead, since the dead are in a different time from ours anyway.

Because of the popularity of *The Tibetan Book of the Dead*, people often think there is something they should be doing during different stages of the death process, but that is just for those who choose to practise in that particular way. Furthermore, we are not going to know what is happening to the dead person or which stage of the process of death and rebirth they have reached. Even if we did, all we would really need to do is keep up our practice according to the various ways I have suggested.

Nonetheless, forty-nine days is a sensible length of time to do intensive practice for someone close to you who has died, because it is long enough to do justice to everyone's feelings of grief and respect. The end of the seven week period signals that it is time to pick up the threads of one's life again.

One way of observing the forty-nine days is to do something special every seven days after the person has died, and then something special on the forty-ninth day. That something special could be extra sessions of meditation, reciting scriptures or praṇidhānas, making extra offerings of candles, and so on. There are no hard and fast rules. People follow their own inspiration. I tend to recommend to my students that they do the feast offering that we do on special occasions. This can be done alone or together with other practitioners, friends, and relatives, and the power of the goodness from it is then dedicated for those who have died. At the feast, people can read things they think the deceased would have appreciated or which might be helpful advice for them.

People often worry whether about they have 'done enough'. This comes from wondering what the person who died is going through, and not wanting to feel helpless. We would like to be able to see them benefiting, and then we would know they were all right. However, we are not going to be able to do this, so we have to content ourselves with just doing our best and then relaxing. From the Buddhist point of view, whatever help we give will help in the long term, even if the immediate effects are unknown. Our calmness and confidence are more likely to help the deceased than a lot of worry. That is for sure.

Calmness and confidence lead to equanimity, and this is helpful for the deceased. This might sound a bit cold and detached, but I mean a loving non-attachment. Non-attachment doesn't mean we don't care. We do care, but somehow we have the confidence to let the person go because we know our deep heart connection that cannot be destroyed is more important than the temporary connections we enjoyed together in life. Trusting in this prevents our being distracted as we practise, and is how we best help the deceased.

Parinirvāṇa Day

This is a day on which Buddhists in some traditions reflect on their own death, or the death of friends and loved ones who have recently passed away. Traditionally, passages are read from the *Parinirvāṇa Sūtra*, which is the scripture that describes the Buddha's last days. For my community of students, I have instigated a similar annual gathering when we focus on death, although it falls on a different day.

Many Buddhists meditate or hold special ceremonies on Parinirvāṇa Day to mark the death of the Buddha. In Buddhist countries, it is often a social occasion where food is prepared and people bring offerings to the monasteries. Buddhist calendars note when this day falls, which is usually in mid-February.

This would be a good time both to reflect strongly on the impermanence of this life for all beings, and to do extra practice to benefit people who have died with whom you are connected. The connection is still there and it can still help them profoundly in ways we cannot imagine.

Animals

From the Buddhist perspective, animals are as much persons as human beings, so everything in this book about humans and death applies equally to animals. Animals go through the same process of dissolution, Clear Light, intermediate state, and rebirth; as Natsok Rangdröl says, the Clear Light 'appears even to the tiniest insect'. We can also benefit a dying or dead animal by practising for them in the same way I have described. Similarly, most of what I say in the next chapter about relieving suffering, ending life, and disposing of the body applies equally to animals. Lastly, as many pet owners have discovered, bereavement at the death of an animal is no different from bereavement at the death of any dear friend.

It is important to think of the animal as not just an animal, but as a being with Buddha Nature who has become temporarily lodged in an animal body. Once it has died, it is unknown what its next birth will be. There is no reason to suppose it will not be reborn as a god, a king, or a great Bodhisattva. From the Buddhist perspective of karma, even a great meditator can temporarily be trapped in an animal body before progressing on their path to Awakening. It is even possible for a great Bodhisattva to take birth as an animal (or any other kind of being) for the benefit of others.

NINE

Practical planning for one's own death

This chapter is primarily for those who are committed to following the path of Awakening. It is a kind of checklist of practical issues that need thinking about in order to prepare for our death as Buddhists. Since some of these issues are quite complex, I will do little more than raise them and make a few suggestions. The selected reading list at the end of the book goes into greater detail.

As Buddhists, we regularly reflect on death as an essential part of our practice. Even so, we may find that we have not thought through what kind of a mess and confusion we might inadvertently be leaving behind for other people to clear up. It is considerate to those we leave behind to have all our affairs in order. Since we do not know when we are going to die, this means getting them in order right away.

Having done this, when the time does come to die we and our loved ones can focus all our attention on connecting to the path of Awakening rather than worry about practicalities such as our will, our wishes in regard to our property, our funeral, and so on.

Planning for your own death

In case we are no longer able to communicate our wishes to others when we come to die, those who are in attendance on us need a means of knowing our wishes in regard to matters such as when to switch off life-support systems, the level of drugs we would like administered, how long we wish our corpse left undisturbed, organ donation, and so on. The document that deals with this is known as a living will.

The need for a living will has arisen because of advances in modern medicine, which can interfere with and unnaturally prolong the natural process of dying, sometimes more or less indefinitely. It helps medical staff, close relatives, and friends to arrive at a sensible decision about what treatment and support to provide.

It would be against Dharma principles to ask to be killed in order to avoid suffering. However, whether all cases of withholding medical intervention are killing is a debatable point. From the Buddhist perspective, when it comes to grey areas like this, each person has to make their own decision based on Buddhist principles. We are not always in a position to know for sure which of a number of possible actions is for the greater good or the greater harm, so we just have to make a choice and accept the consequences. If our motive for making that choice is based on sound principles and proceeds from our heart, this is the best we can do. If there are any negative karmic consequences arising from our decision, we will have to suffer them, but at least we can know that whatever those consequences are, they will be mitigated by the fact that we acted in good faith and with the best of intentions. I would encourage people to consider these issues, and make their wishes known.

If we find ourselves in the position of having to take responsibility for decisions on someone else's behalf, we will have to make our best judgement in the circumstances. All we can do is look at the situation as honestly as we can, taking into account our own motivation and state of knowledge, and make the best choice we can. This is a time to pray for guidance if ever there was one. It is often very helpful to reflect on what you yourself would like if you were in the same position. Pet owners often face difficult issues like these, and the general perspectives I am giving here generally apply for animals as well as people.

In view of all this, making a living will would obviously be very helpful. In this way we take responsibility on ourselves for whatever actions are taken on our behalf at the time of death. More details of how to write a living will can be found in the sources listed at the end of this book.

Similarly, it is important to write a 'last will and testament' that is clear and properly drawn up, in order to minimize any disputes or disharmony after we are gone.

We can use the testament to cover items such as the name of our executor and the dispersal of our personal possessions, whether we would prefer a post-mortem not to be performed, whether we wish to be cremated or buried, the kind of funeral service we would like, whether we would like gifts to be donated to a particular charity or offerings to made to certain teachers or communities on our behalf, and so on.

For practising Buddhists, it is very beneficial to inform our Dharma friends and family of our spiritual wishes in the event of our death. This is something we can discuss with those who are close to us. It can also be a great comfort for those who are practising to feel they are fulfilling the exact wishes of the deceased, but our requests should take into account what they are likely to feel inspired to do. Personally, I would like people to do what they feel most conviction about and dedicate it to me and the fulfilment of my wishes.

Here are some examples of the sort of instructions you might address to those who will be around you and looking after your in your final days.

- Please inform my Dharma Teacher/s […] as soon as possible and follow any advice he or she gives, even if it is contrary to what I have written below.

- I do not want to be kept on a life-support system if medical opinion is reasonably certain that I will never regain consciousness.

- I would like to be given drugs to reduce intense pain, but not ones that make me unconscious when I die.

- I wish to die where my Dharma teachers and/or Dharma friends can stay near me rather than in hospital.

- I wish to donate any of my organs that may be of use to others, and my body to be used for any purpose that advances the cause of medicine or science. Otherwise I would like my body left undisturbed for at least forty minutes after death.

- I would like my remains to be cremated and my ashes left in a place sacred to Buddhists.

- I would like a Buddhist funeral led by my own Dharma teachers or Dharma friends. I would like my relatives and friends to make readings of their choice for me.

- I would like a modest display of flowers at the funeral and for the rest of the money that friends and relatives might have spent on flowers to be used for the following Dharma or charitable purposes: […].

- I would like my Dharma friends to have my name on their shrine and mention my name for forty-nine days when dedicating their regular practice.

- I would like my Dharma friends to do the following practices [...] or whatever practice they feel most inspired by, and dedicate them to me.

- I would like them to do the following practice [...] at the end of forty-nine days and on the first anniversary of my death.

Organ donation and post-mortem

There are various considerations to bear in mind when deciding whether or not to carry a donor card that indicates that you are willing for organs to be taken from your body after you have died and given to others who need them. Many Tibetan Buddhist teachers encourage people to be donors, and it is clearly a form of generosity as it accords with the Bodhisattva vow to sacrifice oneself for the sake of others.

Nonetheless, there are certain considerations from a Buddhist perspective that suggest there is sometimes an element of risk involved. The issue is that the surgeon sets to work removing the organs at most only a few minutes after the heart stops beating, or even while it is still beating in the case of 'brain dead' patients whose heart is sustained by a life-support machine. As I shall explain in more detail later, the actual moment of death from a Buddhist point of view occurs some time after the heart stops beating, usually only moments later but sometimes longer, perhaps hours or even days later. So the question is whether removing organs from a person who is not yet dead, or did not understand they were dead, might cause them pain or suffering.

Most people are attached to their bodies, so there is a danger that if they become aware they are being cut open they might not remember they wished this, and experience anger or suffering. Having asked for clarification on this area from a number of Tibetan teachers and from studying various Buddhist manuals on the subject, my conclusion is that there is no certainty that one would not feel any pain or suffering by having one's organs removed, although the likelihood is that one would not. This is because for most people the dissolution process is so quick.

It is worth noting that not all Tibetan Buddhist teachers encourage the giving away of one's organs, nor do they necessarily give them away themselves at death. For a very advanced practitioner, the time following death is very important in order to benefit others through one's meditation. I have not been able to ascertain exactly how much of a problem it would be for a meditator to have the dissolution process interfered with by the surgeon removing organs before the process was complete.

I make this point about possible suffering because otherwise, if we believe the Buddhist teachings imply that organ donation would not cause us suffering and then we found it did, we would be shocked and lose confidence. At least if we have been warned, we will not lose faith in Buddhist teachings at that important juncture. All sources stress that if we adopt the positive attitude that we are glad to be giving our organs for the benefit of others, and we do not mind any suffering this will cause, we will make positive karma by giving away our organs and this will be of long-term benefit for ourselves and others.

It seems to me that it is always best to be prepared to suffer at death, since none of us knows how we will die. Intrusive though having our organs removed may be, it cannot be anywhere near as bad as all manner of violent deaths that people have to face. Whatever the circumstances of our own death, all we can do is face it with confidence and courage. At least if we choose organ donation we know it is intended for someone's benefit and it is with our permission.

Those around us can help by reminding us of this, so that we feel pleased and don't get angry about what is happening. As always their attitude and calmness will help us to cope, and they could practise tonglen for us.

When you come to choose whether or not to be a donor, there are two fundamental questions you need to ask yourself. First, are you one of the rare people, probably someone who has spent much time in meditation and probably done long retreats, who has recognized your true nature in life and might be able to recognize it at the moment of death? If yes, then it may well be better to avoid organ donation so as not to risk interfering with this important opportunity, which is of such inestimable benefit for yourself and for others. On the other hand, you might well feel confident that organ removal would not disturb your practice at death and, from a deeper understanding than mine, decide in favour.

Secondly, if you are not such a meditator, are you inspired and enthusiastic about giving away your organs even if it causes you suffering? Such Bodhisattva motivation is of inestimable benefit to yourself and others. Alternatively, do you feel more confident and inspired to keep your mind peaceful, so that you don't want to risk any interruption to your Dharma practice from getting upset when your organs are removed. There is a risk (even if slight) that such an interruption at such a moment could affect the nature of our next rebirth. These questions are something we all have to decide on for ourselves, following our own feeling about which way of keeping to the path and benefiting others gives us most confidence.

If you decide you do not want to risk being a donor, you should not feel that this is a problem. It is spiritually dangerous for practitioners to take on more than they can handle and end up regretting a good deed. It is better to admire those practitioners who can do greater deeds than us and aspire to become like them than to regret our good deed and lose faith in the Dharma.

As for a post-mortem, it would seem there is likely to be no more harm in a post-mortem than in any other interference with the corpse once the consciousness has left. In Britain we are perfectly within our rights not to allow a post-mortem, unless for reasons of a criminal investigation. However, since a post-mortem is a means of furthering medical science and it is unlikely to disturb us, there doesn't seem to be any particular problem with it from the Buddhist point of view. To give permission out of a wish to benefit others is a positive thing to do.

Drugs and life-support machines

Modern medical technology provides many ways to reduce suffering and prolong life, and this sometimes raises difficult questions about whether or not it is better to have this treatment. For example, is it good or bad to turn off a life-support machine if someone has no chance of recovering? Is it good or bad to take pain-relieving drugs, even if to do so would hasten death?

One important point is that the Buddhist tradition clearly asserts that intending to kill someone (even oneself) has very serious negative consequences, so it is important to make sure this is not our motive, whatever we decide to do. Obviously this is a dangerous area, as a suicidal person could say it is their suffering and not their life that they wish to end. The points I am making below apply in cases where life is soon to end anyway and there is no chance of it being extended. We are talking here about making that end as painless as possible, not about taking life in order to end suffering.

Modern technologies, particularly life-support machines, have blurred the distinction between taking life and allowing someone to die. However, the Tibetan Buddhist teachers I have asked have all said that if someone is certain to die anyway, and is just being kept suspended in a state of unconsciousness between life and death, then there are no negative consequences from turning off a life-support machine and letting them go on their way.

At some point, there may be a choice between taking more medication to relieve pain with the certain knowledge that this will shorten life, or to allow nature to take its course and cause us a longer period of pain before the inevitable death. In these circumstances, when one is certain to die within hours anyway, it would not generate negative karma to take the medication, providing one's motive were to reduce suffering rather than to end life.

Buddhists sometimes think they should not take painkilling drugs that dull the mind. This is a particular way of interpreting the fifth of the five traditional Buddhist precepts of basic conduct, which is literally against taking alcohol. Such practitioners think that one should try to remain as aware as possible so that one can meditate at the time of death.

Of course, it is good to try to be as clear as possible as one dies, because one can then make sure one has positive thoughts, trusting the heart and dying with a good attitude. Nonetheless, if one's suffering is too intense one might find it impossible to think anything positive and might even become very negative, in which case one might as well take painkillers, even if they make one unconscious.

Generally speaking, we try to do everything we can to avoid pain and discomfort for ourselves and others, but sometimes there is nothing to be done and all we can do is try to adopt a positive attitude and simply bear it as best we can. One could argue that for Dharma practitioners it is good to try to work with pain as much as we can, in order to deepen our practice of patience and equanimity. This trains us to face all experiences with courage and confidence, even when medication is not available or cannot help us. Working with the pain means training oneself not to shrink from it, but to open out to it in a relaxed way, focusing on the actual experience while letting go of all our thoughts about it. This is a very powerful way of meditating if you can do it.

But these days, taking pain-relieving drugs can often make it easier to remain clear, relaxed, and confident as death approaches. Therefore, unless you have trained and gained confidence in meditating on pain, or are inspired to do this at death, I suggest you take medication at death in the same way as you would do in life, to relieve pain and discomfort wherever possible.

Leaving a body undisturbed

As I explained in the previous chapter, in the Tibetan tradition of Buddhism it is thought best to leave a body undisturbed during the period in which the consciousness is losing its connection with the body, the stages of the outer dissolution, the inner dissolution, and the Clear Light. Obviously this issue is of some practical significance for those around a dying person, so I will attempt to explore more the question of just how long a body should be left undisturbed. My basic answer is that in practice this is not something you need to worry about very much, because these processes all happen so quickly. Furthermore, moving a person immediately before their death cannot always be avoided. For example, if the patient is in bed, nursing staff might have to turn them regularly for their own comfort, and this could easily coincide with the moment of death.

During the outer dissolution, the person is still breathing and their heart is still beating. The point at which the heart stops is not the moment of death from a Buddhist perspective. It is the beginning of the inner dissolution. It is better if they are left undisturbed at this time and during the dawning of the Clear Light that comes afterwards.

So in practice the question becomes how we are to know when the inner dissolution and Clear Light have finished. Only a very experienced and realized practitioner could tell directly. However, Natsok Rangdröl in *The Mirror of Mindfulness* explains that both the inner dissolution and the Clear Light usually pass in a matter of moments for most people. For some people, he says, they take somewhat longer, perhaps between five and twenty minutes. He suggests it is rare for the consciousness to stay in the body longer than this, the exceptions being people who have a very strong attachment to their body and adept meditators who can remain stably in the Clear Light for a considerable length of time. So it would seem that normally it is probably safe to disturb the body even within minutes of the heart stopping, and almost certainly after forty minutes.

Tibetans traditionally try not to move the body for three to three and a half days. However, my teacher, Khenpo Tsultrim Gyamtso Rinpoche, says it is fine to handle a body (even cremate it) much sooner than this. Although texts like *The Tibetan Book of the Dead* sometimes talk about the Clear Light lasting three 'days', Natsok Rangdröl emphasizes that these are not ordinary solar days; their duration depends on the mind of the person and they can pass very quickly indeed. Natsok Rangdröl explains (p.53),

> It seems, because of the words used and the intervals and the duration of all that transpires, that these bardo stages appear for a long time, whereas in fact they do not last very long.

The traditional idea that we should leave the body undisturbed for three days would therefore seem to be in part a misunderstanding, and in part a way of playing it safe, as we never know when we might be dealing with the rare cases of someone especially attached to their body or someone who was (perhaps secretly) a great meditator. Just to be sure, you might want to avoid doing anything severe to the body, such as cremation or burial, for three days.

It is particularly significant that experienced practitioners such as Khenpo Tsultrim Gyamtso and Natsok Rangdröl say that most people leave their body only moments after the heart stops, so it is almost certain to be safe to handle the body after, at most, forty minutes, because these days, unless one dies at home, it is rarely possible to leave a body undisturbed for three days. Even if one dies at home, friends and relatives might not be willing to have the body there for that length of time.

What to do with the remains

From the Buddhist perspective, what happens to the corpse or ashes is usually not important, except perhaps for those left behind. So unless the dead person had very strong views and wishes, it doesn't matter how we dispose of them.

The Buddhist traditions generally favour disposing of the body to the lighter rather than the heavier of the four elements (earth, water, fire, and air). Therefore leaving the body out in the open to be eaten by birds and so taken up into the air, or burning it and letting the ashes blow away in the wind, is preferred to burial in the ground or in water. The thinking behind this is concerned with creating auspicious connections. For example, the lightness of the elements air and fire connect with the clarity and space of the Awakened Heart. Bokar Rinpoche (an eminent practitioner and one of my teachers) said,

> *The way we dispose of a corpse has no importance per se if there is no connection with a spiritual practice. Whether you bury, cremate or plunge a corpse in water, there is virtually no difference. In Buddhism, when a corpse is cremated, a ritual called the offering to fire is performed as it helps to burn the errors and the karmic veils of the deceased. In that case, cremation is beneficial and only in this case. Similarly the deceased will benefit if the corpse is dropped in the sea or in a river with the intention of making some kind of contribution to the fish or shellfish or if it is buried in connection with a religious practice. These differences are differences of customs related to the countries and it is right to follow the local customs.* [*]

Although there are a number of references to unfamiliar practices here, the general thrust of the message is clear. We do not have to worry about following a particular method of disposing of the body. We can take whatever method is customary in our

[*] Bokar Rinpoche, *Death and the Art of Dying in Tibetan Buddhism*, pp.114–5

society and make that into something meaningful and beneficial to the deceased by linking it to Dharma in whatever way we feel inspired. This could be a Buddhist-inspired ceremony in which anyone can take part, or it could just be a way of thinking that we adopt in our own mind, if it is not appropriate in the circumstances to do something more public.

Having said this, it is still the case that the remains of the deceased constitute a continuing physical connection with them, so by treating them respectfully we are honouring that connection. One possibility is to have the ashes or remains enshrined in a stupa. A stupa is basically a burial mound or relic container used to mark and hold the power of adhiṣṭhāna and connection between the living and the dead. In Buddhism the stupa is filled with relics of Awakened beings or Dharma teachers and practitioners. The ashes of those close to them are often enclosed with them, and the whole thing is regarded as a sacred place marking the presence of the Dharma in the world. A stupa can be quite small, like an image that you can place on your shrine. One can think of a photograph, clothing, or possessions of a dead practitioner acting in the same way.

The funeral

Ceremonies are very helpful at times of transition, and give meaning and direction at a time when emotions are running high and things can be very confusing. Ceremonies help to acknowledge what is happening and give the transition a very supportive spiritual and social context.

A funeral service can be devised using readings that the deceased and their dear ones find inspiring, incorporating as much Buddhist input as seems appropriate. The family might wish for a Buddhist teacher or practitioner to lead the proceedings to give them a sense of depth and connection with an authentic spiritual tradition.

Funeral or memorial services can take the form of a kind of cele-bration of the life of the deceased, and from the Buddhist point of view this is a good way of helping the deceased understand that, though loved, they are dead and gone and should depart in peace. However, such events are mainly helpful for the bereaved and not much to do with helping the dead.

I find it interesting that in these days, when families have so often become dispersed and seldom meet up, it is funerals rather than any other single event that brings them all together again and again. It is almost as if we still intuit that heart connections are important at death, even though time and distance make it far from obvious why this should be.

The following example service is one I have used on several occasions. I originally devised it for a person who didn't think of herself as a Buddhist, but had strong leanings in that direction, which her friends knew about and respected without knowing much about Buddhism themselves. Her family asked me to visit her shortly before she died, and I talked to her and her daugh-ters about the importance of heart connections that remain even after the body has died. When she finally died, they asked me to do the funeral for them in their field before the coffin was taken to the crematorium.

There were about a hundred friends and family there and I was not sure what they would make of the ceremony, but afterwards many of them came to thank me, saying how they felt the form of ceremony had given them a sense of tradition and rootedness that did justice to the occasion, even though they were not of the same tradition. I felt happy that everyone had had the opportu-nity to make a strong connection to Dharma and that this was all dedicated to the person who had died. Even though I said it was not necessary for them all to join in with the chanting, they joined in with full force, making it a very moving occasion.

Order of Service

Family and friends are invited to join in silent remembrance of the deceased, both as a way of expressing their own feelings of connection, respect and sadness, and as a way of giving spiritual support to the deceased. We then hear from various participants as they share memories, songs, poems, or thoughts connected with the deceased. Finally, the following Buddhist scripture is read and people are invited to join in with the mantra if they feel inspired to do so.

Reading of the Sūtra

The *Heart Sūtra* connects us to the living tradition of Buddhism and expresses the whole essence of the Buddha's teaching on how the ultimate nature of reality (here called Prajñāpāramitā) is beyond conceptual grasping (called here emptiness). This nature unites us all as a single essence and yet we each manifest individually according to our connections. This single essence lies at the heart of our being and, to the extent that each of us can link into that in a genuine way, we link into the heart essence of all beings and bring them support and comfort.

Listen to the recitation of the sūtra as you would an inspiring story. It speaks of a reality that lies beyond birth and death. As the mantra is recited, let your feeling of connection with the deceased link you to all those gathered here in their memory and to all beings. The mantra is an ancient prayer for the ending of suffering and confusion and the dawning of spiritual awakening.

The Heart Sūtra

Thus have I heard.

Once the Blessed One was dwelling in Rajgir, at Vulture Peak mountain, together with a great gathering of the sangha of monks and a great gathering of the sangha of bodhisattvas. At that time the Blessed One entered the samādhi that expresses the dharma called 'profound illumination', and at the same time noble Avalokiteśvara, the bodhisattva mahāsattva, while practising the profound prajñāpāramitā, saw in this way: he saw the five skandhas to be empty of self nature.

Then, through the power of the Buddha, venerable Śāriputra said to noble Avalokiteśvara, the bodhisattva mahāsattva, 'How should a son or daughter of noble family train, who wishes to practise the profound prajñāpāramitā?' Addressed in this way, noble Avalokiteśvara, the bodhisattva mahāsattva, said to venerable Śāriputra, 'O Śāriputra, a son or daughter of noble family who wishes to practise the profound prajñāpāramitā should see in this way: seeing the five skandhas to be empty of self nature.

Form is emptiness; emptiness also is form. Emptiness is no other than form; form is no other than emptiness. In the same way, feeling, perception, formations, and consciousness are emptiness. Thus Śāriputra, all dharmas are emptiness. There are no characteristics. There is no birth and no cessation. There is no impurity and no purity. There is no decrease and no increase.

Therefore Śāriputra, in emptiness, there is no form, no feeling, no perception, no formations, no consciousness; no eye, no ear, no nose, no tongue, no body, no mind; no appearance, no sound, no smell, no taste, no touch, no dharmas; no eye dhātu up to no mind dhātu, no dhātu of dharmas, no mind consciousness dhātu; no ignorance, no end of ignorance up to no old age and death, no end of old age and death; no suffering, no origin of suffering, no cessation of suffering, no path, no wisdom, no attainment, and no non-attainment.

Therefore, Śāriputra, since the bodhisattvas have no attainment, they abide by means of prajñāpāramitā. Since there is no obscuration of mind, there is no fear. They transcend falsity and attain complete nirvāṇa. All the buddhas of the three times, by means of prajñāpāramitā, fully awaken to unsurpassable, true, complete enlightenment.

Therefore, the great mantra of prajñāpāramitā, the mantra of great insight, the unsurpassed mantra, the unequalled mantra, the mantra that calms all suffering, should be known as truth, since there is no deception.

Thus, Śāriputra, the bodhisattva mahāsattva should train in the profound prajñāpāramitā. Then the Blessed One arose from that samādhi and praised noble Avalokiteśvara, the bodhisattva mahāsattva, saying, 'Good, good, O son of noble family; thus it is, O son of noble family, thus it is. One should practise the profound prajñāpāramitā just as you have taught and all the tathāgatas will rejoice.'

When the Blessed One had said this, venerable Śāriputra and noble Avalokiteśvara, the bodhisattva mahāsattva, that whole assembly and the world with its gods, humans, asuras, and gandharvas rejoiced and praised the words of the Blessed One.[*]

Reciting the Mantra
oṃ gate gate pāragate pārasaṃgate bodhi svāhā

(*Oṃ*, gone, gone, gone beyond, gone altogether beyond, Awakening, so be it)

---

[*] Lotsawa Bhikshu Rinchen De translated this text into Tibetan with the Indian pandita Vimalamitra. It was edited by the great editor-lotsawas Gelo, Namkha, and others. This Tibetan text was copied from the fresco in Gegye Chemaling at the glorious Samye vihāra. This translation into English is a slightly modified version of a translation by Francesca Fremantle.

Invoking the power of the truth

In the Buddhist tradition, as in our own folk tradition, it is believed that words of truth spoken from the heart have the power of fulfilment. In this spirit we recite the following:

Through the power of the truth of the true nature of our
being,
The indestructible essence of the heart,
Though the power of the truth of our inherent qualities
Of openness, clarity, and sensitivity,
Through the power of our inescapable connection with each
other
And the all-pervading truth of the Buddha,
Through the power of all the good that we have done,
Do, or ever will do,
May you and all beings always find your way on the path to
Awakening,
Without fear, obstacle, or hindrance.

May you be protected from fear – be relaxed and fearless
May you be protected from grasping and clinging –
remember everything passes
May you be protected from anger and hatred – let go of
everything good or bad.

With thoughts full of love and joy,
Thinking of how we will all meet again and again,
Determined to repay the kindness of all beings,
And repair all the harm we have ever done or will do,
May you pass in peace from this life into the next.

The Committal

The committal is the portion of the service in which the remains are actually committed to the elements (e.g. sent rolling into the furnace at a crematorium, or lowered into the ground in a burial). At a Christian burial service the traditional words for the committal are, 'earth to earth, dust to dust, ashes to ashes,' and so on. As an example, here is the text I used at the cremation of a non-Buddhist friend whose wife was a Buddhist.

This body is merely the shell of the spirit that lived within it. That spirit has now gone and is experiencing another world, another life, another magical display of illusion. Yet the essence of —'s being remains within our hearts. It is in our hearts that we come to know this, the profoundest of mysteries. Our connection with — and with each other does not die when our bodies die. Our connection, the connection that we feel and know in our hearts, is not of the nature of what dies. It is constant, and it is in this constancy that we put our trust, as we commit his body to the flames. We take the inspiration of his life into our life, living our life for the benefit of others in whatever way we can and as he would have been glad to see.

TEN

Bereavement

In this chapter I talk briefly about bereavement and related issues. The reader will need to look at books that deal specifically with bereavement, some of which I recommend in the suggested reading section, for a more thorough treatment of this important subject.

Intense bereavement is about as close as we can possibly get to experiencing death and groundlessness outside of death itself. It can thrust us into a frightening no man's land similar to the intermediate state between death and rebirth. We can find ourselves suspended between past and future, suddenly cut off from all our associations with the deceased, having to die to our old way of life, and feeling we have lost our self and our identity.

If it's true that this is like dying, then the experience of bereavement can be a terrible but an amazing gift, a wake-up experience, a Dharma practice. Many people have noticed this deeply spiritual dimension to bereavement.

There are of course various levels of bereavement, depending on one's degree of attachment and closeness to the dead person and how much he or she was integral to one's sense of well-being and feeling loved. But any bereavement can be an important Dharma practice, because at the very least it brings us face to face with our own mortality. That in itself is a shock and can be

Bereavement

hard to handle, especially if it is something we have never really related to before.

The shock of death

A big part of the suffering of grief either before or after a dear one's death is brought on by shock. In Tibetan culture, this condition is described in terms of the life-force (*tsolung* in Tibetan). It is said that the life-force, or subtle energy of the body, which usually functions and moves in the heart, is severely blocked owing to shock. I think the custom of beating one's breast, familiar from many cultures, clearly reflects a similar understanding of the need to get the life-force moving again. While it is blocked (as also happens in depression), one's whole will to live drops away, everything appears colourless and meaningless. Even to perform the simplest of functions involves a tremendous effort. There is very little point in trying to talk about the meaning of life to someone in this condition. There is no energy or inspiration in one's thinking and, in fact, it is important not to think too much at a time like that.

Anything that gets the life-force moving, such as physical exercise, walking, massage, or just pottering about, are good for someone in this condition; in fact, anything that keeps one moving, but doesn't take too much thinking or energy. Light-hearted but sensitive company is a tremendous help. This is where pets, family, friends, and especially the support of fellow practitioners and spiritually like-minded people can play an important role.

It is good to set yourself a routine that keeps you moving without getting frantically involved in lots of things. There is often a lot to do when someone dies, and it is likely to be a very busy time. This can take one's mind off things for a while, which provides some much needed movement, but when all the busyness dies down, one should not be surprised to find that it can take a very long time for the life-force to recover. It often happens that everyone is very attentive around the funeral and for the first month or so after the death of a loved one. About three months after that, when the death has become more real, the bereaved seem to need more help, and it is often just at this time that most friends and family have withdrawn.

It is very helpful if one can somehow feel the heart connection one has with the deceased person and learn to trust that. It re-affirms the value of a person and our connections at a time when we are very open to the true essence of what that means. Doing things for the deceased at that time helps reinforce the sense of connectedness. Meditation, offerings, praṇidhānas, mantras, tonglen, feasts, and dedicating the power of our practice (*puṇya*) for the deceased, as well as talking to them, can help the person doing these things as much as it helps the deceased. The more faith one has in all these practices the better, but even simply being open to the possibility that there is meaning in them helps the heart. It helps one feel there is a power in the universe that cares, and that there is a truth and dignity inherent in a long-standing spiritual tradition that feels supportive and inspires confidence. This can be true even if one is not sure one can go along with all the implied beliefs. The reassurance this gives the bereaved helps counter the overwhelming feeling of meaning-lessness that is likely to descend on them. It provides some sense of groundedness without which it is very hard to recover.

I believe the whole process of recovering the life-force can take several years, but it does recover, and during that time it tends to chop and change. Sometimes it seems to have picked up energy, and sometimes the energy drops again apparently for no reason. Knowing this is likely helps us to face it with courage. It is very important to turn towards and acknowledge what is happening, and to let it be, without complicating things by thinking one should be able to do better.

Developing spiritual understanding in grief

After a bereavement, people often turn to Tibetan Buddhist teachers for support. I have to warn you that you might simply be told not to grieve. I think what Tibetans mean is that we should not think too much in a way that clings to the past and drags us down. They certainly understand as well as we do that it is important to be gentle with ourselves and give time and attention to helping the life-force to recover.

Perhaps it is a question of what we mean by grieve. It can be taken to mean just feeling sorry for oneself. However, grief can also refer to the whole process of recovery from the shock and pain of being bereaved. This is not self-indulgence. It is a very important stage in our life and we need to use the time of grief, however long it takes and in whatever form, as a means of taking our understanding to new depths and finding an inner strength we hardly knew was possible. To do this we need to acknowledge and allow ourselves to fully experience the different stages of the grieving process. So the instruction not to grieve should not be taken to mean that we should suppress our feelings and pretend nothing is happening.

Tibetans often have very strong faith, which makes a huge difference. If you have that kind of trust in the path of Awakening, it is sometimes hard to appreciate how bereft someone who is relatively new to the practice of Dharma can feel. For many of us, our confidence in Dharma is like a delicate young bird that has barely learned to fly. It is important not to make ourselves feel even worse by blaming ourselves for not being further along the path than we are. This kind of trust is something that dawns slowly in its own time. So be gentle with yourself.

For all of us, the death of a loved one and the grief that follows tend to bring an urgency to questions about the meaning of life and death. It may even help inspire us to look deeper into our being to discover the true nature of our being. Our sense of the meaninglessness of saṃsāra intensifies, so that as and when it becomes possible, we are gently able to stop clinging to the saṃsāric parts of our experience and learn to trust the Awakened Heart within ourself and the deceased, whom we love so much. It is necessary to allow yourself to turn towards the turmoil of the grief experience, including all the emotions of anger, betrayal, guilt, sorrow, fear, feeling overwhelmed, isolated, desolate, and so on. You learn from the whole experience as long as you turn towards it all. If you just try to let go of all the negative feelings and move on as if nothing had happened, you cannot really use the experience to gain in spiritual strength and understanding. But if you turn towards the emotions, you can learn something about your heart, and therefore about your heart connection with the deceased. This allows you to really honour your connection with the deceased. From a Buddhist perspective, having this kind of attitude of heartfelt openness is the best way to strengthen your connection with a person who has died, so that you meet again and again in future lives in a way that benefits you both.

Having said this, for a Dharma practitioner, it can sometimes come as a shock that, after someone has died, when one thinks one should be practising more than usual, one finds it almost impossible simply to sit and meditate. It is important not to be hard on oneself about this because actually, when the life-force is blocked, it is important to keep moving and maybe it is the right instinct to fight shy of just sitting. Of course, if one finds one can sit and still gain inspiration from it, it is a wonderful thing to do at that time. However, if one finds it is just not like that, do not worry. Instead it is good to do walking meditation, or what I call pottering meditation. By this I mean find little tasks to do around the house or garden that you can do in a relaxed and meditative way. You may find it is easier to recite mantras than to meditate, just because they involve movement and give you a bit of energy to keep the mind positively focused. It is even better if you can recite them with deep trust in the heart and a sense of the presence of the supportive power of Awakened beings.

Bereavement is a time when we are able to feel the underlying suffering of saṃsāric existence very acutely, and this joins us very intimately to the whole of humanity. Recognizing this, and perhaps doing the tonglen practice for all people everywhere who are suffering bereavement, can help us to let go of self-concern and feel less lonely. All those who are not grieving now have this suffering to come. All those with loved ones have to suffer this way at death, if not before, and to have no loved ones to lose is a grief all of its own. There is no way saṃsāra can be made to add up to happiness in the end. The Buddha taught the truth when he pointed out the path that leads beyond birth and death as the only way.

Being kind to yourself in these circumstances to give yourself as much time as necessary to reflect quietly, without the pressure of thinking you should be over this or doing better. It's a matter of just noticing what is happening, reflecting, and making aspirations and wishes on behalf of your loved one, yourself, and others.

Another way of looking at the grieving process is that it is quite humbling. In one's desperation and despair, one's pride and ego-clinging are crushed and one's tender heart is exposed. This feeling of raw exposure cannot be avoided; it is the essence of our being, open, aware, and excruciatingly sensitive. So much is this the case that we want to dull it out and not feel it. But we do. So intense grief is actually a wonderful opportunity to move forward spiritually, painful though it feels at the time. It is the Awakened Heart itself that is hurting, and that is the essence of our life, our being, our compassion, love, and joy. Eventually we need to learn that we can let go of attachment and egocentric clinging and simply survive with an open and hurting heart. Sometimes it may seem that to let go of attachment is to let go of love, but it isn't. The love remains, deepens, and expands. Our heart opens more and we realize it is bigger than the little self that was so afraid. The little self thought it could not bear the grief, yet our heart can bear it. It is actually indestructible and even the pain is simply an expression of its indestructible nature. It is in the sensitivity of our true nature, and by turning towards it and – in a sense, dare I say – welcoming it, one discovers it is actually the essence of compassion. Given time, from within it, an appropriate response arises spontaneously. Life goes on.

Through experiencing the suffering and loss of bereavement, we can find that our spiritual path can deepen in ways previously unimaginable, and we can connect with our fundamental openness, clarity, and sensitivity with greater confidence. Our relationship to others and to life can be transformed. In our heart of hearts, we all wish that our life had this kind of effect on our loved ones. Allowing their death to deepen and strengthen us spiritually is the finest way to honour the deceased, to express what they meant to you, to help them, and to strengthen your connection with them.

Supporting the bereaved

As I mentioned earlier, some levels of grief are more difficult to work with than others. If someone has only ever experienced a death that has been expected for a long time, or the death of an aged relative, they cannot automatically expect to understand someone going through grief such as that arising from the sudden death of a spouse or partner, a suicide, or the death of a child, and they are apt to try to make that person 'move on' long before it is possible or desirable.

It is insensitive to try to get the bereaved to 'move on' or 'let go', in what may feel like an insulting and heartless way. When people do this it is probably their own feelings of fear, inadequacy, and impatience talking. Somebody who has been through the same suffering themselves is more likely to be able to respond sensitively than others, but it all depends on the person. If that person has been insensitive to themselves in bereavement, they are likely to be insensitive to others.

It can be helpful to talk to the bereaved about what others experience in similar situations, and how long it takes them to recover. I don't mean in a 'this is what you should do' way, but in a way that allows the bereaved to feel they are not unusual and to feel reassured by others' experiences.

The bereaved need to have a lot of patience with those around them, just as those around a bereaved person often need to have a lot of patience with them. Everyone has their own problems associated with the death of a loved one. Some people, in spite of what has happened, might actually be trying to push the whole idea of death out of their mind, and to put any reminder of death behind them as soon as possible. For such people the bereaved person's pain is uncomfortable and an embarrassment.

The most important thing to remember when confronted with a person who is suffering grief (or suffering in any way, for that matter) is to be supportive while encouraging them to find their inner strength and their own way of dealing with it. This means not approaching the situation with a preconceived idea of what the person is experiencing and a whole agenda of your own about how they should deal with it. It means being open and supportive without thinking you have to approve or disapprove of what is going on. You don't need to communicate your personal judgement. They need to feel they have the space to explore what they are experiencing, and for that very little is needed from you except to be there and listen, and respond with love and understanding.

The bereaved often want to talk about the illness or accident that caused the death of their loved one, and even about the death itself, in great detail, almost blow by blow, as if saying the words out loud will stop them going round and round in their head. They also often just want to talk about the person who died and what they meant to them. Since other people are likely to want to shy away from listening to this, it can be very helpful and supportive to just be there to allow the bereaved person to share their experience with you. When we do this, we create a kind of space in which the person who needs to talk doesn't feel they have to worry about being attacked or offending anyone, so can expand into that spaciousness and find their own response to the situation. It might come as a shock to us that our advice is not actually needed, but it is wisest not to advise unless you are absolutely sure you are being asked for advice.

Though many people will be able to find their way through the often long and difficult grieving process with the help and support of friends, some may also benefit from the help of a grief support group or a professional bereavement counsellor, especially after a particularly intense experience of a loved one's death. A professional counsellor can be called for if the grieving person talks of suicide, stops eating, or totally isolates themselves, and certainly if they stop caring for themselves or their family. The best way to find a bereavement counsellor is through a hospice. There are many counsellors out there who are not qualified to deal with bereavement, but a hospice will know those who are fully experienced with the care of the dying and bereaved.

Some people want to be left alone with their grief, and I think it is important to respect that and not insist that they should express or show their grief in some prescribed way. For example, some people consider certain ways of behaving, such as crying, healthy. But some people cry, and some don't. There is nothing wrong with not feeling like crying or not wanting to talk about things. It all depends how one is with that, and that really only shows over time. Again, it is important not to have a preconceived idea of what is the right or wrong way to grieve.

We can support others, even if we don't quite understand what they are going through, just by being there and allowing the person concerned to communicate to us what they are feeling and want. That way, we are more likely to respond sensitively and appropriately.

ELEVEN

Reflecting on death throughout life

Having written a whole book for others on the topic of death, my intention now is to use it to reflect on death again and again myself. As I said at the outset, even though the theme of death is central to Buddhism, it is amazingly hard to keep it well in mind.

Traditionally, a Buddhist teacher would give a student the practice of reflection on death as a preliminary before engaging in any other practice, such as meditation or study. From then on, the student would be expected to spend time reflecting on death every day of their life. When you read the lives of the greatest practitioners, those who have succeeded in Awakening, it is clear that they reflected deeply on death, and that was what motivated them and enabled them successfully to traverse the path to Awakening. This reflection provides both the vision and the impetus to overcome all difficulties, and to regard any difficulty on the path as nothing compared with the pain of remaining trapped in the unawakened state of saṃsāra.

So I suggest from time to time setting aside five minutes to an hour to think about the inevitability of death. Don't think to yourself that you don't have time for this; you can do it walking down the street. In fact, it is very effective to do it in a crowded street thinking about how every single one of the people you see is going to die. What is even more awful is that none of us knows when. Any one of those people, even we ourself, might be the next to go.

When we hear about the danger of terrorism, we tend to feel very threatened and may think, 'Oh, I don't want to go to London or New York, or fly in an aircraft. I might get blown up.' But terrorism only raises the probability of our dying today by a tiny fraction. We might die today anyway. There is absolutely no security. So there is something poignant about everyone getting upset about some particular disaster somewhere in the world; it is as if we are ignoring the fact that the whole of life is a disaster. We act as if just this one little bit of the whole thing is a disaster and how dreadful it is that people have to suffer that. But in fact we are all in the situation of not knowing which of us is going to have to suffer next and in what kind of way. Terrible and fatal illnesses strike young and old, rich and poor, high-fliers and society's outcasts with equal disregard for status or person.

As we try to focus on this, it is interesting how strongly we resist this way of thinking. There is only any point to it if we have some kind of confidence that there is a path that leads to Awakening.

As we get older and see young people looking so happy and confident, so pleased with their looks and attractiveness, we remember the time of our own youth when we, like the young today, couldn't really imagine becoming old. All the evidence was there, but we ignored it. Of course, we all know intellectually that we are getting old and death is drawing nearer all the time, but we act as if death is far away. Very old people seem like a race apart. Even as we grow old, we are constantly trying to tell ourselves we are not really that old. It is as though we are being taken on a train to a place of slaughter but we keep telling ourselves, 'Oh no, I am just on a sight-seeing tour,' refusing to think about where the train is going.

This is like the father of the Buddha-to-be trying to hide the true nature of life. The story goes that he hoped that if his son never thought about old age, sickness, or death, he would not give up worldly ambition. He wanted his son to seek worldly success and knew that if he saw what was really in store for everyone, he would lose all that ambition. There is a strong side in all of us that is like that father, trying to persuade us things are really not all that bad. If we forget that it is going to the place of our death, it can be fun, in a narrow, limited way, to be on this train that is our life. It is so easy to forget all about the destination and just to enjoy the ride; or at least simply try to make the journey as comfortable as possible, instead of seriously thinking about getting off the train altogether. To get off the train altogether would be to find the essence of pure enjoyment, but we do not see it that way.

That is why it is necessary to reflect again and again on the fact that all worldly joy ends in suffering and death, and that the Buddha opened a way to the joy of Awakening that goes beyond all suffering, birth, and death. It is only by reflecting on this again and again, and by repeatedly reading the accounts of accomplished practitioners, that we realize that what is being said here is extremely relevant and important. You might even find reading this page again and again a good lead in to this kind of reflection.

It is important, as we reflect on the inevitability and unpredictability of our death, to also reflect on the lives of the Buddha and his followers down the ages, and what they discovered. We need to have some sense of the possibility of there being an alternative path for us, otherwise reflection on death is just depressing or could even induce a devil-may-care attitude. If we are all going to be dead soon, why not just grab as much pleasure as we can, while we can?

Often the most accomplished practitioners have the message of death and suffering thrust on them by life's circumstances while they are still young. From the Buddhist perspective this is a great blessing. It caused them to realize very early on that saṃsāra holds no hope, and prepared them for their Dharma journey without misgivings. The rest of us have to reflect again and again to really bring home the message that death could happen any time and that it is coming nearer all the time. Otherwise, even though we see and hear of people's deaths all the time, we still regard death as something that happens to other people, while our own continues to seem remote.

The need to reflect on death

The Buddha's path means giving up attachment to all we are holding on to. It means giving up our cherished views about ourselves and the world. This can be as scary as death itself. In order to find the courage to be able to make that leap, we need to realize just how dangerous the situation in which we find ourselves is. For example, one might be very frightened about jumping out of an aircraft with a parachute. However, if you were aware that the plane was on fire and was about to crash, it would be much easier to find the courage to jump.

An advantage of having reflected on death very strongly again and again is that we are more able to open to our own and others' deaths. We are not trying to pretend it is not happening or it couldn't happen, and we are not seeing the dying person in a category apart. This is already very helpful for a person who is dying.

Another important point about reflection on death is that, as we open to it, the more obvious it becomes that our whole world could collapse any time. This opens us up to realizing the ungraspable nature of reality, emptiness. To experience this suddenly in meditation can be very frightening, like death itself. We quickly want to grasp onto our life and world, and perhaps do not want to go near the path to Awakening again for a while.

Some people sense that if they were to look too carefully at the nature of the world they are attached to, they would lose interest in it and somehow become alienated or different from their friends and family. These kinds of fears often stop people wholeheartedly pursuing the path to Awakening. These and other deep-seated habits of mind cause us to cling to this world and neglect to follow the path to Awakening, even if we are vaguely inspired by it. We try to convince ourselves that saṃsāra is really not that bad, life is oĸ, we don't really need to give up attachment or, at least, not all of it, not yet. But when we reflect deeply on death we realize that this is just deception, and that we need to gather the courage to face that deception and the fear that gave rise to it, in order to dare open our hearts and turn towards our true nature.

It is easy to have doubts, thinking that maybe the whole idea of Enlightenment or Awakening is a pipe dream or a fantasy. Deep reflection on death, however, can help us cut through this kind of doubt. At death, it is certain we will be cut off from all we cling to in this life, but there is no evidence to suggest awareness itself will die. The more we look at the nature of awareness, the more we realize it is not of the nature of something that dies. This realization, combined with the recognition that death severs us from all we cling to in life, makes reflection on death our dearest friend. It is the friend that drives us into the arms of our own salvation.

The best preparation for death

Trusting the heart is trusting what is real. Recollection of death stops us investing too much in what is unreal, so that at the time of death we can let it all go. If we have an attitude of continuously recollecting that death can strike at any moment, this gives us a realistic perspective on life and its problems, and inspires us to practise Dharma and take full advantage of the present opportunity to do so. That is how to die without regret.

Anyone who has thought about the inevitability of death and developed the habit of letting things go will suffer less at the time of death. This is an attitude we can encourage everyone to adopt towards life and the things of this life they may be attached to.

Natsok Rangdröl quotes an authoritative text (p.34):

> *All people feel attachment to their possessions—*
> *To children, cattle, and wealth;*
> *'That I have done, now I do this.*
> *When this has been done, I will then do that.'*
> *While people are thus being fooled by distractions,*
> *They depart, snapped away by the Lord of Death.*

At its deepest level, remembering death and impermanence is the gateway to realizing the emptiness of what we take to be real, and the undying quality of what is truly real. By constantly remembering death and impermanence, we become increasingly aware of the dream-like and illusory nature of our life and experience, so that it does not come as such a shock when we are confronted with death. The deeper we realize this truth, the more prepared for death we are, and the nearer to Awakening.

Turning the mind away from saṃsāra

Death comes without warning!
It may come today,
Parting me from all that is familiar
And all those I love.
Now is the time to think
Of what heart connections mean.
Now is the time to think
Of what goes beyond birth and death.
Now is the time to discover
And learn to trust
The Openness, Clarity, and Sensitivity
Of my being,
The Indestructible Heart Essence of all beings.
I have today to prepare.
Worldly attachments are useless,
As are anger and delusion.
Now is the time to let them go
And rest relaxed in my own true nature.
What use am I to others
If I am no use to myself?
How can I liberate them
If I cannot liberate myself?
May I and all beings be happy
And have the causes of happiness.
May I and all beings be free from suffering
And the causes of suffering.
May I and all beings have the happiness of complete
    Awakening
That will never diminish or fail.
Thus may we abide in great equanimity,
Unruffled by attachment and aversion
And with equal love for all beings.

Written by Lama Shenpen Hookham for the benefit of students
attending a meditation retreat in the autumn of 2002.

Suggested reading

Buddhism and death

Judith L. Lief, *Making Friends with Death*, Shambhala Publications, 2001. Judith Lief is a Buddhist teacher. In this book she shows us that by honestly contemplating death and using mindfulness practice, we can change how we relate to death, enhance our appreciation of everyday life, and open ourselves to others.

Christine Longaker, *Facing Death and Finding Hope: a guide to the emotional and spiritual care of the dying*, Arrow, 1998. Christine Longaker is a student of Sogyal Rinpoche and has devoted her life to learning how, with compassion and wisdom, we can ease the suffering of those facing grief or death. In this book she draws on Tibetan Buddhist teachings for guidance in preparing both emotionally and spiritually for death – for ourselves and for others – and shows how by so doing we transform our relationship with life. She emphasizes that these spiritual principles are universal, enabling readers of other spiritual traditions (or none) to find resonance in their own innate wisdom.

Tsele Natsok Rangdröl, *The Mirror of Mindfulness: the cycle of the four bardos*, Shambhala Publications, 1989. A classic of Tibetan literature, containing instructions on how to deal with death and the intermediate state and attain Enlightenment.

Sogyal Rinpoche, *The Tibetan Book of Living and Dying*, Rider, 2002. This book deals with the topic of death from many points of view, and links it to the importance of practising formless meditation. He goes into more detail about the dying process than is necessary, but this is not an essential part of the book. He assumes a very devotional approach to the teachings, with a lot of emphasis on relying on a master. It is important to notice that wherever he talks about his master he is talking about all his teachers generally, and he encourages everyone to rely on whoever or whatever they have most faith in. Many people find the simple powa practices that he suggests on pp.214 onwards very helpful.

General books on death and bereavement

The following books discuss the experience of death and bereavement and seek to give a spiritual, though not necessarily Buddhist, perspective and are strongly recommended by Buddhists who have deeply contemplated death.

Elisabeth Kübler-Ross, *On Death and Dying*, Simon & Schuster Inc., 1997.

Elisabeth Kübler-Ross, *Death: the Final Stage of Growth*, Simon & Schuster Inc., 1997.

Steven Levine, *Who Dies?*, Gateway, 2000.

Steven Levine, *Healing into Life and Death*, Gateway, 1989.

Judy Tatlebaum, *The Courage to Grieve*, William Heinemann, 1993.

Ken Wilber, *Grace and Grit*, Gateway, 2001.

Cicely Saunders, *Living with Dying*, Oxford University Press, 1995.

C.S. Lewis, *A Grief Observed*, Zondervan Publishing House, 2001. I would strongly recommend this small book in which C.S. Lewis records his feelings and thoughts more or less day by day as he comes to terms with his grief at the death of his beloved wife. Above all it is an examination of what we mean by a person. It is not a cloud of atoms of disconnected events that end at death. A person is a mystery outside time and space, maybe a 'super-cosmic eternal something', and what we get attached to in a person is simply a place where the spheres of our beings momentarily intersect. We cannot see or sense the rest of it; that living sense of communication that exists in that fleeting moment of intersection leaves us longing for more. I think what C.S. Lewis's intuitions and insights are reaching out to is what I have been describing in terms of the Awakened Heart and the mysteriousness of our being: personal and yet ungraspable Openness, Clarity, and Sensitivity.

Other resources

A good place to find up-to-date and more comprehensive information about books and useful websites on Buddhist approaches to death is the Spiritual Care Program founded by Sogyal Rinpoche. Their website is www.spcare.org

An excellent website for all manner of practical information on subjects like living wills, pain management, and hospice care is www .growthhouse.org. This information is largely USA-focused; for information on legalities in the UK, visit www.ifishoulddie.co.uk or www .direct.gov.uk/RightsAndResponsibilities/Death

Glossary

Adhiṣṭhāna (Sanskrit; Tibetan *chin lab*) Literally 'influence' or 'possession', but often translated 'blessing' or 'grace'. This is the power that flows out from something. The most powerful and beneficial source of adhiṣṭhāna is the Buddha and the reality he embodies.

Awakened Heart (Sanskrit *bodhicitta*; Tibetan *chang chub sem*) The innermost nature of all beings that underlies all our experience. This term is used particularly when talking about our ability to Awaken, and how this nature can stir and propel us to seek a path that leads us and all beings out of saṃsāra.

Awakening (Sanskrit *bodhi*; Tibetan *chang chub*) The goal of the Buddhist path, Enlightenment, liberation from saṃsāra.

Bardo *see* Intermediate State.

Bodhisattva (Sanskrit; Tibetan *chang chub sempa*) Someone with the determination to awaken to full Buddhahood for the benefit of all beings. Technically it refers to beings who have realized emptiness, met the Buddhas face to face, and made a vow in their presence to bring all beings to Awakening. Less technically, it is applied to anyone who aspires to follow this path and has made a formal commitment to doing so.

Bodhisattva Vow In general use it is the vow to follow the path to Awakening for the sake of others rather than for oneself. Technically, it is the vow to realize full Buddhahood in order to work for ever to liberate all beings and bring them to the same stage of perfection. It also involves taking a vow to train and to accomplish all the deeds of the Bodhisattvas for the benefit of beings.

Buddha (Sanskrit; Tibetan *sanjay*) Someone who has fully Awakened. This includes not only the historical Buddha of ancient India who founded the Buddhist tradition, but a limitless number of other beings from other worlds and times who have also Awakened.

Clarity (Tibetan *salwa*) One of the three inseparable qualities of the true nature of reality (especially in the Dzogchen and Mahāmudrā traditions). As such it is used synonymously with awareness and refers to the brightness of awareness that, like a mirror, has the power to make manifest the world of our experience.

Clear Light (Sanskrit *prabhāsvara*; Tibetan *ösel*) Another way of referring to the essential nature of reality. This term is particularly used when talking about the fundamental nature of mind, awareness, or experience. It is revealed at death, when all else dissolves. 'Clarity' or 'luminosity' might possibly be better translations.

Dharma (Sanskrit; Tibetan *chö*) Dharma is used to mean truth or reality, with the understanding that it is what the Buddha discovered when he Awakened and then taught, revealed, and demonstrated to others. It has come to be used synonymously with the path to Awakening, so we talk of practising Dharma, meaning following the path to Awakening. But since it also means the reality revealed at Awakening, the living Truth of the universe that is drawing us to itself, we also talk of Dharma as a force in its own right, rather than simply a path that we follow.

Dzogchen **(Tibetan; Sanskrit *Mahāsandhi* or *Atiyoga*)** Literally 'great perfection', 'great completion', or 'great finishing'. A term from the Nyingma or old school of Tibetan Buddhism that arrived in Tibet with Guru Rinpoche, if not before. It is the highest possible realization beyond even the notion of Awakened and Unawakened, and another name for reality itself. It is often used as though it were the name of a practice, e.g. practising Dzogchen. This is a loose way of talking about practising in a way that will lead to the realization of Dzogchen. The Dzogchen tradition means the teachings from the lineage of teachers who have realized Dzogchen. It has its own traditions, techniques, terminology, transmissions, and so on. Although it is principally thought of as a Nyingma tradition, yogins from other lineages, especially the Kagyupas, also practise and transmit it.

Gandharva **(Sanskrit)** A being undergoing the intermediate state between death and rebirth.

Intermediate state (Sanskrit *antarabhāva*; Tibetan *sipa bardo*) An unstable state of existence entered into at death which lasts until entry into a stable rebirth. It is characterized by volatile experiences like dreaming, with no connection to a stable world to wake into, such as one has in life.

Karma (Sanskrit; Tibetan *lay*) Literally 'action'. Although it refers to our volitional actions that have inevitable consequences for us in this and future lives, the term is commonly used to refer to the consequences themselves, especially in the way they manifest as happiness and suffering in this life. The consequences of actions performed in one life may lie dormant for lifetimes and 'ripen' more or less at random. This means that none of us knows what actions are going to ripen next, so happiness and suffering unremittingly follow each other until we escape the trap of saṃsāra.

Life force (Tibetan *tso lung*) The prāṇa that moves in the heart and keeps us alive and keeps our spirits up. Shock, grief, anxiety, and loss of confidence can block it, and this manifests as various kinds of mental and physical distress.

Mahāmudrā **(Sanskrit; Tibetan *Chagja Chenpo*)** Literally 'Great Symbol or Seal' in Tibetan. Although this is a term used in the Dzogchen tradition for a level of realization that falls short of Dzogchen, it is used by the Kagyu tradition, synonymously with Dzogchen, to indicate reality or Awakening itself. This has led to endless discussions about whether or not Dzogchen and Mahāmudrā are the same. The third Karmapa (Rangjung Dorje, fourteenth century) unified the Kagyu Mahāmudrā and the Nyingma Dzogchen traditions into one system. So Kagyupas tend to hold that Dzogchen and Mahāmudrā are the same.

Mahāyāna (Sanskrit; Tibetan *tekpa chenpo*) Literally 'great vehicle'. The Buddhist teachings that lead to complete and perfect Buddhahood. Mahāyāna sūtras refer to themselves as Mahāyāna, and contrast these with teachings that lead to a goal short of complete and perfect Buddhahood. The main issue here is that it is possible to Awaken to a kind of Enlightenment that does not awaken to the subtlest and deepest meaning of the Awakened Heart that enables us to develop the full knowledge, love, and powers of Bodhisattvas and of complete and perfect Buddhas. These powers are of immense benefit to others, which is why the Bodhisattva vows to attain them.

Mantra (Sanskrit; Tibetan *ngak*) A Buddhist mantra is a set of sounds (syllables or words in a spell-like form) that expresses the essence of a particular Awakened being and which invokes their presence. The adhiṣṭhāna of that being is made to flow through repeated recitation of the mantra.

Nirvāṇa (Sanskrit; Tibetan *Nya ngan lay day*) Nirvāṇa is the opposite of saṃsāra. It is the cessation of suffering. It is the reality that the Buddha Awakened to and therefore the true nature of reality, of the universe, of everything. It is often referred to as peace and as the heart's release.

Openness One of the three inseparable qualities of the true nature of reality (especially in the Dzogchen and Mahāmudrā traditions). As such it is used synonymously with emptiness (Sanskrit *Śūnyatā*; Tibetan *Tongpa nyi*). It refers to the ungraspability of awareness which, like space, is changeless and indestructible.

Prāṇa (**Sanskrit; Tibetan** *lung*) Literally 'wind' or streams of living energy within the body which are inseparable from the mind.

Praṇidhāna (**Sanskrit; Tibetan** *mon lam*) Often translated rather inadequately as 'wishing prayer', it is more powerful than just a wish, although it is essentially the power of our volition empowered and made effective. Maybe it is not so much what we would call a prayer as what we would call a clearly formulated blessing (or curse). When somebody powerful utters their word of truth with one pointed concentration and conviction, this is a praṇidhāna and it has the power to fulfil itself. For example, 'may you be well,' 'may the gods go with you,' 'may I gain Enlightenment for the sake of all beings.'

Puṇya (**Sanskrit; Tibetan** *sonam*) Often very weakly translated as 'merit', it refers to a power that comes from good actions that can be accumulated and used to accomplish our praṇidhānas.

Pure Land (**Sanskrit** *buddhakṣetra*; **Tibetan** *shing kam*) A world created by the *puṇya*, *praṇidhānas*, and *samādhi* of a Buddha that is designed for the benefit of beings so that they may enter it at the time of death and thus make rapid progress on the path. Many Buddhists focus their practice more or less entirely on the aspiration to enter such a Pure Land, and dedicate all their puṇya and make constant praṇidhānas to accomplish this end.

Refuge 'Taking refuge' is the commitment to follow the path and teachings revealed by the Buddha. It can be done informally through reciting a liturgy or simply by being committed to the Dharma and the path to Awakening. When refuge is formally taken from a preceptor at a ceremony, it marks a definite decision and moment of being received within the community of followers of the Buddha.

Saṃsāra (**Sanskrit; Tibetan** *khor wa*) Literally 'the turning'. It refers to the turning or wandering round and round in an interminable succession of lives characterized by suffering. It is existence as experienced by unenlightened beings, whether it's the treadmill of living from day to day, going nowhere except into old age and death, or the suffering of being trapped in delusion from one life to the next.

Sangha (**Sanskrit; Tibetan** *gendun*) Literally 'assembly'. (The Tibetan equivalent literally means 'longing for virtue'.) The community of the followers of the Buddha. In Buddhist countries it is often used to refer to the community of monks and nuns, but technically in the Mahāyāna tradition it refers to the community of Awakened Beings who lead others to Awakening. Once the Buddha had disappeared from this world, the Sangha became responsible for transmitting the Dharma from one generation to the next. These days in the West it sometimes refers to any body of Buddhist practitioners who develop a sense of spiritual community.

Sensitivity One of the three inseparable qualities of the true nature of reality (especially in the Dzogchen and Mahāmudrā traditions). As such it is used synonymously with responsiveness, and refers to the same inseparable quality that in Tibetan is called bliss (*day wa*), compassion (*tuk jay*) or unobstructed play (*ma gag*). It refers to the living responsiveness inherent in awareness, such as a sense of well-being in the heart that gives value to experience.

Sūtra **(Sanskrit; Tibetan** *do***)** Texts that are accepted as having been spoken by the Buddha, or spoken in his presence and approved by him. Thus these are the principal authoritative source for the teachings within the Buddhist tradition. There are various collections of sūtras, some in Pali (used by Theravādin Buddhists), and some in Sanskrit and Chinese. The Chinese were particularly prone to call important texts within their tradition 'sūtras', even when there is no suggestion that they were spoken by the historical Buddha or in his presence. The point is that the teaching is the authentic Dharma and carries the adhiṣṭhāna of the Buddha, the Awakened One. The Mahāyāna perspective is that the true sūtra is a spiritual revelation of something that exists, in some timeless sense, forever, and can be entered like a kind of world by any being who has contact with it at any level. Hence sūtras are treated as sacred objects, almost like people, in many Buddhist traditions.

Buddhism Connect

If you would like a regular dose of inspiration from Lama Shenpen, you can subscribe to Buddhism Connect. This is a free online service that sends out a short teaching from Lama Shenpen every few days by email.

Many people have described these emails as a lifeline in the midst of their busy lives. Getting an email of Buddhist reflection and advice can remind you what is most important, helping you to reconnect to your heart and inspiring you to keep pursuing your meditation. The teachings are short and practical, usually with Lama Shenpen answering a student's question about meditation or how to practise amidst daily life or difficult situations.

- There's no charge (although donations are welcome).

- To join the Buddhist Connect email list, just go to
www.buddhism-connect.org

- You will receive a short teaching by email every few days.

- You can easily unsubscribe from the list at any time if you want to stop receiving the email teachings.

- Your privacy is protected – your email address is never shared or sold.

The best way to find out what it's like to is to try it. You can always unsubscribe if you decide after a few days that you're not interested.

Discovering the Heart of Buddhism course

Lama Shenpen created Discovering the Heart of Buddhism as a training for people who want to explore the practice of Buddhism in a direct, authentic, and systematic way. It is aimed both at those who have practised Buddhism for some time and those who are completely new to it. Structured course books introduce the core themes and prompt you to apply them to your life.

•Engage in a comprehensive and structured experiential training in Buddhist study, reflection, and meditation.

•Discover the truths of Buddhism through your own experience. All you need is an open and inquiring mind.

•Connect to the heart of Buddhist teachings without the confusion often caused by Eastern cultural trappings.

•Receive regular guidance from the teacher and senior students who have studied for years in the Mahāmudrā and Dzogchen traditions of Tibetan Buddhism.

You can find out more and enrol at the website:
www.buddhism-connect.org

The Awakened Heart Sangha is a spiritual community formed by students of Lama Shenpen. For any general enquiries please email us at info@ahs.org.uk

The windhorse symbolizes the energy of the Enlightened mind carrying the truth of the Buddha's teachings to all corners of the world. On its back the windhorse bears three jewels: a brilliant gold jewel represents the Buddha, the ideal of Enlightenment, a sparkling blue jewel represents the teachings of the Buddha, the Dharma, and a glowing red jewel, the community of the Buddha's enlightened followers, the Sangha. Windhorse Publications, through the medium of books, similarly takes these three jewels out to the world.

Windhorse Publications is a Buddhist publishing house, staffed by practising Buddhists. We place great emphasis on producing books of high quality, accessible and relevant to those interested in Buddhism at whatever level. Drawing on the whole range of the Buddhist tradition, our books include translations of traditional texts, commentaries, books that make links with Western culture and ways of life, biographies of Buddhists, and works on meditation.

As a charitable institution we welcome donations to help us continue our work. We also welcome manuscripts on aspects of Buddhism or meditation. For orders and catalogues log on to www.windhorsepublications.com or contact:

Windhorse Publications	Consortium	Windhorse Books
11 Park Road	1045 Westgate Drive	PO Box 574
Birmingham	St Paul MN 55114	Newtown NSW 2042
B13 8AB	USA	Australia
UK		

Windhorse Publications is an arm of the Friends of the Western Buddhist Order, which has more than sixty centres on four continents. Through these centres, members of the Western Buddhist Order offer regular programmes of events for the general public and for more experienced students. These include meditation classes, public talks, study on Buddhist themes and texts, and bodywork classes such as t'ai chi, yoga, and massage. The FWBO also runs several retreat centres and the Karuna Trust, a fundraising charity that supports social welfare projects in the slums and villages of India.

Many FWBO centres have residential spiritual communities and ethical businesses associated with them. Arts activities are encouraged too, as is the development of strong bonds of friendship between people who share the same ideals. In this way the FWBO is developing a unique approach to Buddhism, not simply as a set of techniques, but as a creatively directed way of life for people living in the modern world.

If you would like more information about the FWBO please visit the website at www.fwbo.org or write to:

London Buddhist Centre Centre	Aryaloka	Sydney Buddhist
51 Roman Road	14 Heartwood Circle	24 Enmore Road
London	Newmarket NH 03857	Newtown NSW 2042
E2 0HU	USA	Australia
UK		